Country Chuckles, Cracks & Knee-Slappers

Edited By Mike Lessiter

Lessiter Publications, Brookfield, Wis.

Publisher's Cataloging in Publication
(Prepared by Quality Books Inc.)

Country chuckles, cracks & knee slappers / edited by Mike Lessiter.
p. cm.
Includes index.
ISBN 0-944079-02-4

1. Wit and humor--United States. 2. Country life--United States.
I. Lessiter, Michael J.

PN6157   808.882
                                     QBI91-1417

International Standard Book
Number: 0-944079-02-4.

Library of Congress Catalog
Card Number: 91-76821.

Published by Lessiter Publications,
a divison of No-Till Farmer, Inc.
P.O. Box 624, Brookfield, Wisconsin 53008-0624.
Manufactured in the United States of America.

Cover Design: *Greg Kot*

*We proudly dedicate this book to the
thousands of farmers who have
mailed us their favorite jokes over the
last half-century so we could share them
with country people everywhere.*

*We hope you enjoy the following
pages—we sure did.*

The First Laugh

Old Joe was hauling a load of manure down the country road when he met an inmate from the neighboring county mental institution.

"What are you going to do with all that manure?" the inmate asked.

Joe replied, "I'm going to put it on my strawberries."

"And they call me crazy," the inmate said, shaking his head. "I put sugar and cream on my strawberries."

—*Earl L. Butz*

Now...A Word About This Book!

DURING A long-term career in agriculture that has covered more than seven decades and let me talk and joke with farmers all over the world, I've always noticed that farmers never seem to lose their sense of humor.

They've lost livestock, lost crops, lost farms, lost faith in the weather, lost dollars on market reports, lost family members, lost their marbles, lost livestock, lost money, lost their shirts, lost meals and lost practically everything else that comes to mind. But even with all these terrible kinds of disasters, farmers have never seemed to forget how to smile.

As a result, farmers are blessed with that great ability to laugh at themselves and to find many funny things in almost any situation that makes carving out a living from the soil so worthwhile.

Nobody can deny that farmers are a fun-loving bunch of people who really like to smile. And if they couldn't smile, they sure wouldn't have any business putting up with all the problems, risks and gambles that go with farming today.

By its nature, a farm serves as a very funny environment. Animals, farm workers, pets, family members and farm machinery all seem to have unique and quirky personalities. Many have been captured in this exciting book of country humor that you now hold in your hands.

The stories that appear in this book found their way into the "Farm Funnies" pages of *Farmer's Digest* magazine over the past 50-plus years. They represent the very best that country humor has to offer. In fact, I've already spotted some great farming and ranching stories in this book—including a number of tales I've been lucky to share with farm audiences all around the world. As a result, I know these stories will get a good laugh from you and other country folks.

So sit back, enjoy this book and let the laughs flow freely. With all that has been happening recently in agriculture, you certainly deserve a good belly laugh.

—Earl L. Butz

Ag Dean Emeritus, Purdue University
U.S. Secretary of Agriculture, 1971-76

Another Laugh

A farm magazine editor ran into one of his readers at a field day and they began discussing the editor's sense of humor. "Do you think I should put more fire into my jokes?" the editor asked.

"No," answered his reader, "I think you should put more of your jokes into the fire!"

Your Page-By-Page Guide To Gut-Busting Laughter

Section 4...A Day With The Animals   53

Section 5...Weather-Beaten   85

Section 6...Courtship   91

Section 7...'Till Death Do Us Part   99

Section 8...Children—Our Bundles Of Joy   127

Section 1

All In A Day's Work

"My father taught me to work;
he did not teach me to love it."

—*Abraham Lincoln*

Chapter 1

Sleeping On The Job

"Hard work won't kill a fellow if he can stay far enough away from it."

☞ A farm hand was showing his friend around the farm. "How long have you been working on this farm?" the friend asked.

The farm hand answered, "Since the boss threatened to fire me."

☞ "You're the laziest person I ever met," the farm manager screamed at a young hired hand. "I don't believe you do an hour's work in a month. Tell me one single way in which the farm benefits from having you here."

"Well," replied the youth after some consideration, "when I go on vacation, no extra work will be expected of the others."

☞ The boss-man scolded Homer, "You're 30 minutes late again! Don't you know what time we start work around here?"

"No, sir," Homer replied. "They're always working when I get here."

☞ Two city boys had just taken jobs as hired hands out in the country. One afternoon, they were napping on the hay bales stacked in the barn.

"Hey, Howard," one said, "I wonder if it's raining right now."

The other boy didn't move and with his eyes slightly open said, "Why don't you call in the dog to see if he's wet."

☞ While fixing the fence, the farmer turned to his hired hand and said, "Do you believe in life after death?"

"Yes, I suppose, sir," the hired hand said.

"Well, that explains everything then, I guess," the farmer said.

"Why?" asked the worker.

His boss replied, "Well, about an hour after you left to go to your grandfather's funeral yesterday, he stopped by to see you."

☞ A foreman saw his laziest worker loafing again and asked, "Why are you carrying four bricks when all of the other men are carrying eight?"

The worker replied, "I guess it's just because all the other guys are too lazy to make two trips."

☞ Throughout his 30 years at the feed mill, Fred earned a well-deserved reputation for his "can do" spirit. You see, whenever there was work to do, he was in the "can."

☞ After getting chewed out by the boss, Pete asked Al, "Why did you tell the boss what time I came in this morning?"

Defensively, Al said, "I did not!"

"Who did then?"

"I don't know," Al answered. "When he asked me, I said I didn't notice because I was too busy getting ready to go to lunch."

☞ A farmer threw a nickel toward the blind man's cup. The coin missed and rolled along the pavement toward the gutter, but the man with dark glasses quickly recovered it.

"Hey, I thought you were blind!" the farmer shouted.

"No, I'm not the regular blind man," he said. "I'm just taking his place while he's at the movies."

☞ Two farmers were talking about their sons. One of them said, "Man, my son is so slow, it takes him an hour and a half just to watch *60 Minutes*."

☞ Although times are changing, this is still the land of opportunity, where anybody can grow up, lose a job and go on unemployment compensation.

☞ "Now for the last time," growled the farm supply manager, "I want to see nothing but people working! I hope everyone knows how this can be accomplished."

"Yes, sir," replied one worker. "Call before you come next time."

☞ While Bobby was playing next door, Mrs. Johnson said, "I'm sorry to hear that your dad was injured on the farm last week. When will he be able to return to work?"

Bobby answered, "Not for a long time. Last night he said compensation had set in."

☞ The store manager, checking the job reference of an applicant, asked the man's former employer if he was a steady worker.

"Steady?" came the reply. "Why, he was practically motionless."

☞ The new farm hand was awakened at 4:30 a.m. by the farmer, who announced they were going to cut oats. "Are they wild oats," the farm hand asked.

"No, of course not," said the farmer. "Why?"

"Then why do we have to sneak up on them in the dark?"

☞ A farmer was talking with his new hired hand's wife and said, "Well, it looks to me like your husband has been fired from every job he ever held."

"Yes," the loyal wife replied, "but it does prove one thing. He's no quitter."

☞ A farmer was giving his son, Judd, the usual lecture. "Why don't you get a job?" he bellowed.

"Why?" Judd asked.

"You could save some money and put it in the bank," his dad explained.

"Why?"

The farmer was growing angry. "When you had saved enough, you wouldn't have to work."

Judd said, "I'm not working now."

☞ Chuck was complaining about work again. "The boss told me yesterday that I'd get a raise when I earned it," he said. "He's crazy if he thinks I'm gonna wait that long."

☞ It's not nice to say one of your workers is lazy. Let's just say that when it comes to burning ambition, he could be classified as flame retardant.

☞ A shaggy old man set himself up in front of the town's largest office building with a tray of shoelaces. Each day when an executive passed by he gave the unfortunate man a dime, but he never took the laces.

One day, the peddler, upon receiving the dime, tapped the departing executive on the back and said, "I don't like to complain, sir—but the laces are now 20 cents."

☞ As the movers bumped around the house as they carried boxes out to the truck, the lady said snobbily, "Be careful carrying that dish! It's 2,000 years old."

To which the moving man answered, "You can depend on us. We'll be as careful as if it were brand new."

☞ A scraggly man in a soiled t-shirt was sprawled out on his sofa, watching TV. His wife stormed in and said bitterly, "I don't know why I married you. You look like such a bum."

He peered up at her and retorted, "Oh yeah? And who brings home the unemployment checks?"

☞ You see a lot of new kinds of dolls at Christmas time. We have mechanical dolls that walk, talk, sleep, wet, burp, stretch, roll over and emulate countless other human traits. But now, manufacturers have now come up with the ultimate, called the "Welfare Doll." Wind it up and it doesn't work.

☞ A hillbilly woman said her husband's idea of saving money was not to work hard enough to need deodorant.

☞ At the rural art show, the artist told a man, "I believe in realism. Here is my latest painting. It's called 'Men at Work.' It's modern realism."

"But," the man argued, "those men aren't working."

"That's right," the artist said. "That's why it's so real."

☞ "I always accomplish a lot on Friday," a man was heard bragging to a co-worker.

The boss appeared and snapped, "That's because that's when he finally gets everything done he was supposed to do on Monday."

☞ A farmer was heard talking at the tavern, "My daughter's boyfriend claims he makes a living by the sweat of his brow.

All I can say is that someone should turn down the thermostat in that unemployment office."

☛ A farm wife was overheard at the beauty parlor speaking of her son, a farm hand, who had to quit his job because of sickness. "Sickness?" she was asked. "What happened?"
She replied, "His boss got sick of him."

☛ Vernon had a reputation for being the laziest man in town. When someone asked how they knew he was the laziest, his neighbor replied, "Lazy? Vern's so lazy that last night he called up a singles' bar and asked if they'd deliver."

☛ The farm equipment salesman hadn't been feeling well and was constantly having trouble getting up in the morning. He asked his physician to prescribe some pills. He took one that night, slept soundly, and was awake before the alarm went off.
He had a leisurely breakfast, got to the office and told the boss, "I feel great. I had no trouble getting up this morning."
"Wonderful," replied the boss. "But where've you been the last three days?"

☛ The speaker said, "Tonight we honor a man, who throughout his 30 years at the co-op, was never too busy to see anyone. Well, that was because he was never too busy."

☛ Gordo filled out an application for a job as a hired hand. The farmer looked over the form. Then he said, "I see you have no experience at farm work."
"Yeah, that's right," Gordo said.
"But you're asking for $400 a week," the farmer said. "Isn't that a lot of money for someone with no experience?"
"I don't think so," Gordo said. "The job is bound to be a lot harder when you don't know what you're doing."

☛ It finally came to the point where a rural couple had to discharge their cleaning lady. As she stormed out of the house, the woman pulled a $5 bill from her purse and threw it to the family dog.
"Why did you do that?" the woman of the house asked.
She replied, "I never forget a friend. That was for helping me clean the dishes all these years."

14

Chapter 2

The Boss

"If you do all the work and somebody else gets the credit — he's probably your boss."

☞ As the new hired hand was being introduced to the other farm workers, he asked one, "Is your boss as mean as I've heard?"

"Yeah, he's mean," Bill said. "But he's fair."

"How's that?" he asked.

Bill answered, "He's mean to everybody."

☞ Neil was describing his boss to a friend at the local diner. "Man, he's so screwed up that if he drowned, you'd have to look for him upstream."

☞ A feed mill boss in dire need of workers was interviewing a number of young applicants. After a good prospect named Jim left dejectedly, one of the mill's workers asked his boss why he didn't hire him.

The boss replied, "I asked him what he could do and he said, 'Nothing.'"

"Oh, that explains it," the mill worker mumbled to himself. "If there's one thing the boss hates is somebody who's after his job."

☞ A farm employed a number of young workers during the summer. On their salary receipts was the message: "Your salary is your personal business—a confidential matter—and should not be discussed."

One worker, while signing his receipts, added, "Don't worry, I won't mention it. I'm as ashamed of it as you are."

☞ A farmer and his new hired hand were working on the new barn. "I'm putting this rivet in the correct position," instructed the farmer. "When I nod my head, hit it real hard with your hammer."

When he woke up in the hospital, that's all he remembered.

☞ Our boss is something of a conservative. He still thinks an obscene gesture is reaching for your paycheck.

☞ During the annual farm tour, a visitor asked, "And you say everything on this farm is run by electricity?"

The hired hand answered, "That's right. Even the wages give you a shock."

☞ A good farm manager is one who never puts off until tomorrow what he can get someone else to do today.

☞ A boss noted for his energy and lack of tolerance for loafing visited his stockroom one day and found a boy leaning idly against a packing case, whistling as if nothing was on his mind. The boss stopped and stared.

"How much are you getting a week?" the boss demanded.

"Me?" the startled boy answered. "Ah, about $150."

"Here's your $150. Now get out! You're through!"

As the boy pocketed the money and departed, the boss turned to one of the employees and demanded, "Since when has that fellow been with us?"

"Never, that I know of," was the response. "He just delivered a package from the printer."

☞ "I've been working here eight years now," complained the hired hand to the ranch boss, "and I've been doing the work of three men. Now I want a raise."

The rancher objected. "I can't give you a raise," he said. "But if you'll tell me who the other two men are, I'll fire 'em."

Chapter 3

Another Day, Another Dollar

"Most people don't mind going to work—it's the long wait until quitting time that irritates them."

☞ After his first day on the job, a man hired to paint yellow lines down the middle of the road reported to his foreman that he had painted a three-mile line. The foreman was impressed since a good day is usually two and a half miles.

The second day, the man reported to his foreman that he had added only two miles to the line. "Well," said the foreman, "you have good days and bad days."

But the next day, the worker added only one mile to the line. "I'm sorry," said the foreman, "but each day you paint less and less. We're going to have to let you go."

The man turned to the foreman and yelled, "Well, it's not my fault. Each day I get further from the can."

☞ A woman called the builder of their new house to come over and examine the poor workmanship.

"It's the most poorly-constructed thing I've ever seen," she complained. "The vibrations are so bad that when a train goes by four blocks away it nearly shakes me out of bed. Just lie there and you'll see!"

The contractor scoffed at her but accepted her challenge. He had just stretched himself out on the bed when the woman's husband came home.

"What are you doing in my wife's bed?" he demanded.

The poor contractor trembled. "Would you believe that I'm waiting for a train?"

☞ A man was filling out a job application form at the feed mill and came to the question: "Have you ever been arrested?"

His answer was "No." The next question was "Why?" and

was meant only for those who answered the first question affirmatively.

Nevertheless, he answered it with, "Never got caught."

☛ One afternoon a stranger came into the milking parlor and asked if he could be given a job for evening and weekend milking. The farm manager asked him if he could milk.

"Done a lot as a boy, you know," he assured him.

"During your milking work, have you ever had trouble with mastitis?" the manager questioned.

"No sir," he said, "but I do get rotten colds."

☛ At her first day at the office, the boss told his new typist, "Now I hope you thoroughly understand the importance of punctuation."

"Oh, yes, indeed," the stenographer answered. "I always get to work on time."

☛ The little man applied for a job on the docks as a stevedore. "You're too small," said the foreman.

"Please, give me a chance," the little guy pleaded.

"OK," agreed the foreman. "We're loading 300-pound anvils in the hold of that ship. Get to work."

For a few hours, everything was going fine. Then the foreman heard a splash and a yell for help. Running to the gangplank, he saw the little newly hired helper bobbing up and down in the water.

"Help!" called the little man as he went under. He came up spluttering, called for help again, and went under. The foreman watched and laughed.

"Help!" he yelled as he came up for the third time. "Throw me a rope or so help me, I'll drop this anvil!"

☛ The first grader became curious about her father working in the farm office every night. Her mother explained, "Daddy has so much to do that he can't finish it all during the day. That's why he has to work at night."

"Well, then," the child said, "why don't they put him in a slower group?"

☛ A frustrated farmer who was waiting for his hired hand to arrive picked up the phone. "Boss, this is Joe," the voice said. "I won't be able to come to work today. My wife broke a leg."

The farmer said, "So what's that got to do with you coming to work?"

Joe said, "It was my leg she broke."

☛ The hardware store manager was looking over an application and said, "Look here, what did you mean by telling me you had five year's experience when you've never even had a job before?"

"Well," the young man said, "you advertised for a man with imagination."

☛ A Women's Lib mail survey arrived at the county extension agent's office. The purpose of the survey was to see if female agents were as well paid as male agents.

The survey asked the office to give: "salaries of all agents broken down by sex."

Two weeks later, an old-timer agent wrote back, "None of our agents are broken down by sex, but we do have two that have a drinking problem."

☛ Two men were trying to measure a flagpole. After they made guesses that differed considerably, a bystander asked, "Wouldn't it be better to pull out the pole, lay it down on the ground and measure how long it is?"

"No," one of the men said as he stared in disbelief. "We're trying to figure out how tall it is, not how long."

☛ For many years a rancher employed a fine Chinese cook. After a particularly delicious dinner the rancher raised his wages. The next day, the cook noted the extra money in the envelope. "Why you pay me more?" he asked.

"Because you've been such a good cook all these years," replied the boss generously.

After thinking it over a while, the cook said, "You been cheating me long time, 'eh?"

☛ Two hired hands were discussing their moonlighting jobs. One said, "I work in the opera in town at night and carry a spear in one act."

"How do you manage to keep awake so late at night after working on the farm?" his friend asked.

"Simple," he replied. "The guy behind me carries a spear, too."

19

☛ An agricultural scientist, applying for a position at the Cape Canaveral Space Center, was asked to give three good reasons why he was qualified for the job.

"Well," he answered, "three, I have a graduate degree. Two, I keep cool in emergencies. And one, I know how to count."

☛ A farmer asked a job applicant, "Do you lie, cheat, steal or come in late?"

The anxious young kid answered, "No, I never have. But I can learn."

☛ A old man walked up to an imposing home and asked the lady for a job to earn a hot meal. "It just happens that I have two gallons of paint," said the lady. "If you'll paint the porch out back, I'll see that you get all the dinner you can eat."

Two hours later, the man reappeared at the door, covered in green paint. "Well, I finished the job," he said. "But that's no Porsche, lady, it's a Ferrari."

Trading Places

"There's no place like home."

—Judy Garland in "The Wizard of Oz."

Chapter 4

Cowboys Vs.
City Slickers

"A farmer makes his money in the country and blows it when he comes to town."

Country

"In my hometown, the population is eight. No, make that six. One guy died last week and I'm out of town."
—*John Campbell*

☞ A reporter from a big city newspaper stopped in a rural community to visit a friend who ran a country weekly.

He asked his friend, "Why do people in your town keep buying your newspaper when they already know what everybody in town has done that week?"

The rural editor grinned and pointed out, "They know what everybody's doing all right, but they read the paper to see who's been caught at it."

☞ Two guys were talking about the small towns they came from. One said, "The town I came from was so small that when they had a Christmas parade there was nobody there to watch it—everybody was in it."

The other said, "Shucks, that's nothin'. The town I came from was so small we didn't even have a regular drunk. Everybody had to take turns."

☞ A definition of a rural town is one of those backward places that uses money instead of credit cards.

☞ A couple bought a new television set and the installer drove out to their home in the backwoods to install it. "Now," he said, "this antenna will have to go on the roof."
"Like I said, Ma," the husband sighed, "one thing leads to another. We bought the TV, now we have to build a roof!"

☞ One farmer was overheard at the Farm Bureau Convention, saying, "My hometown was so small that the head of the Mafia was Filipino."

☞ A small town is a place where everybody knows whose check is good and whose husband isn't.

☞ One farmer told his neighbor, "My hometown was so small that it was located on the highway between the third and fourth 'Burma Shave' signs. I had to leave town to read the whole sign."

☞ There's a guy from a town that's so small that his parents got the prize for the first baby of the new year—and his birthday is in June.

☞ There may not be much to see in a rural community, but what you hear makes up for it.

City

"My neighborhood was so tough you'd see guys bowling overhand."
—Rodney Dangerfield

☞ Cities are places where they cut down all the trees and name streets after them.

☞ A farm boy was listening to his cousin talk about growing up in the big city. "What makes you think your schoolmates are so tough?" the farm boy asked.

His cousin replied, "Well, for one thing, the school paper has an obituary column."

☞ A city is a place where a man spends a dollar to park his car so he won't be fined $15 while spending 75 cents for a nickel cup of coffee.

☞ Grandpa observes, "There's no need for a farmer to retire and move to the city. If he stays put, the city will soon come to him."

☞ A man was telling a visitor on the subway about the city. "I'm not so worried about the crime in our streets," he said, "but in our neighborhood, they make house calls."

☞ There was a day when it used to be the ambition of almost every man to go into the country and raise pigs. Now it seems his ambition is to go into the city and raise hell.

☞ Grandpa was always glad to get back from a visit to the big city. "A place without trees," he declared, "isn't fit for a dog."

☞ A city dweller was describing city life to his brother, who lived on a farm. "Yeah, my city claims to be the worst in the nation for crime," he said. "It's gotten so bad that if you go into a department store and order a pair of nylon stockings, the clerk will ask you for your head size."

☞ One man was talking about his cousin. "My family lives in a very rough neighborhood," he said. "For instance, my cousin, Vince, is the oldest living graduate of his class. Now that may not seem like much to you, but he graduated last June."

Chapter 5

A Visit To The Country

*"There's a little country
in all of us, a little frontier."*

—*Louis L'Amour*

☞ A city visitor asked an old farmer about his cows. "Why," he asked, "do some of them have no horns?"

"There are three cases," the farmer said. "Some are born without horns, some are dehorned and some knock their horns off fighting."

"And what about that one in the corner?" the visitor asked.

"Ah," said the farmer. "That is a fourth case. That is a horse."

☞ Little Theodore was a city boy who had never seen a horse and watched with interest as an old-fashioned milkman in a horse-drawn carriage stopped to deliver milk to his grandmother's house.

After dropping off the day's milk, the milkman returned and climbed into his wagon but the horse wouldn't budge. "Of course he won't go," said Theodore from the porch. "While you were gone he lost all his gas."

☞ A brand new farm hand from the city was told to harness a mule one winter morning in the early hours. In the dark he tackled a longhorn steer instead of the mule. The farmer shouted from the house, "Say, what's keeping you so long?"

"I can't get the collar over the mule's head," the farm hand shouted back. "Both his ears are frozen stiff!"

☞ Little Molly visited her uncle's farm last summer and after begging for hours, her uncle finally took her to see the cows being milked.

At supper that evening when her mother noticed the glass of milk at Molly's place was left untouched, she said, "Molly, why didn't you drink any milk?"

In a low voice, Molly whispered to her mother, "Mother, if you knew where it came from you wouldn't drink it either."

☞ A city slicker was taking his first camping trip in the West. "What happens," he asked the cowboy, "if one of those rattlesnakes should bite me in the arm?"

"Don't worry, son, one of your friends will just cut open the fang holes and suck out the poison," he said.

"What happens if I get bitten on the leg?" the nervous man asked again.

"Same thing, son."

"But suppose I should sit on one of them?" asked the nervous city dude.

"Son," the cowboy said, "that's when you'll find out who your real friends are."

☞ Just after the clocks were set back for standard time in late fall, a man stopped for gas at a rural service station in Arkansas.

It was about five o'clock in the evening and already starting to get dark. As the grizzled owner filled the gas tank, the man casually remarked, "I hate it when daylight savings time ends, and we take an hour off. Don't you?"

"Well," he replied, "out here it stays light until it gets dark, so it doesn't make much difference."

☞ A little boy was struggling along the edge of a country road, leading a huge cow. A motorist from a nearby big city thought the boy was having a problem and pulled to a stop.

"Where are you going with that animal?" the traveler asked.

"To the bull down at the next farm," the boy answered.

"Can't your father do that?"

The boy looked at the man strangely and said, "No, sir, I think it has to be the bull."

☞ A city motorist was having his gas tank filled at a lonely country gas station before driving into the mountains. Just as he was about to pay, the gas station attendant took out a ladder and began to change the price of gas on the sign.

"Hey, I'm no fool, you're going to give me the old price on gas, old man," the obnoxious driver shouted, pounding his fist on the desk.

"Have it your way," the station owner said, taking his money, "but the price just went down three cents a gallon."

☛ Andy was out in the barn milking the family's only cow when a load of city folks came driving up. A man got out of the car and came in and asked what time it was. Andy put his head down, grabbed the cow's udder and said "It's about six o'clock."

"Hey, guys, this guy can tell time by holding a cow's udder!" the man yelled to the others in the car. "How do you do it?"

Andy answered, "Come and sit down and I'll show you."

The city man sat down and Andy told him to push up the udder. "A little higher, a bit higher—good," Andy said. "Now, do you see the clock on the wall over there?"

☛ The dairyman's 10-year-old nephews from the city followed him into the milking parlor. They watched him approach the first cow and deftly attach a pair of suction devices.

As he did so, one of the youngsters said excitedly, "Wow! He's going to jump start her the way Dad does!"

☛ The visiting city tenderfoot, about to take his first horseback ride, was checking out the horses at the stables.

After he selected his horse, the old wrangler asked whether he wanted an English or Western saddle. "What's the difference?" asked the tenderfoot.

"Waaal, the English saddle is flat, while the Western saddle has this here horn in the front," replied the wrangler.

"Better give me the English saddle, then," said the visitor. "I don't expect to be riding in traffic anyway."

☛ During the war, an overbearing English woman strolled into a British barn where a young man was milking a cow. With a snort she asked, "How is it you are not at the front, young man?"

"Because, madam," answered the milker, "there ain't no milk at that end."

☛ During the summer farm tours, a city boy asked the farmer, "Where did you take a bath?"

The farmer answered, "In the spring."

The boy said, "I figured that, but I asked where, not when."

☛ The little city boy was on his first real vacation with his father. The two were hiking in the mountains when Daddy pointed out a brilliant rainbow. "It sure is pretty," said the youngster. "What is it—advertising?"

☛ A city salesman was driving down a rural route, and he had to go to the bathroom in the worst possible way. He looked for a gas station or small town, but without any luck.

Finally, he stopped along the side of the road and desperately raced to a farmer who was plowing the field. He explained his situation to the farmer and he told the visitor, "Just run up to our outhouse there at the edge of the farm. But remember one thing..."

The salesman didn't hear him because he was already sprinting for the outhouse. The farmer began to chase him, but he couldn't catch him or make him hear his warning. About 15 feet in front of the outhouse, the salesman ran into a washline. It hit him in the neck and twirled him around three times.

"Sorry," said the farmer. "I meant to warn you about that."

"That's OK," the salesman said. "I don't think I would have made it anyhow."

☛ A city man turned farmer called up the county extension agent and asked, "How long do you have to leave the rooster with the hens to get fertile eggs?"

As the county agent's other phone rang, he said, "Just a minute."

The city slicker said, "Thank you" and hung up.

☛ A city dweller was spending his first week on the mountain dude ranch. He left the ranch one morning to view the countryside, but returned shortly after, all battered and bruised with his clothes torn. "What happened to you?" demanded a ranch hand.

"A little black snake chased me," he answered.

"Those little snakes aren't poisonous," the cowboy laughed.

"Listen," said the vacationer, "If he can make you jump off a 50-foot cliff, he doesn't have to be!"

☛ A city slicker driving through a small mountain town screeched to a halt and shouted to an old-timer sitting on a bench, "Hey, Rube! What time is it?"

"Twelve o'clock," replied the old man.

"Are you sure?" snapped the driver. "I thought it was later than that."

"Don't never get no later than that around here," drawled the old man. "When it gets to 12, we start all over."

☛ Chuckie was visiting his grandparent's farm for Christmas. Watching his grandpa milk the cow in a cold barn one morning, he said, "Grandpa, why don't you put anti-freeze in the cow's radiator so you wouldn't have to drain her so often?"

☛ Deciding to raise chickens on her suburban acreage, Mrs. Smith placed some eggs under a hen and then asked how long before she could expect them to hatch. "I believe," said her neighbor, "that the rule is 21 days for chickens and 23 for ducks."

Later the neighbor inquired as to what luck she'd had. "Oh," said Mrs. Smith, "when they did not hatch on the 21st day, I sold them. I didn't want ducks."

☛ A New York tourist ambled into a small town blacksmith shop and picked up a horseshoe without realizing it had just come from the forge. Dropping it quickly, he put his sizzling hand in his pocket and tried to appear nonchalant.

"Kinda hot, wasn't it?" asked the blacksmith.

"Nope," said the New Yorker. "It just doesn't take me long to look at a horseshoe."

☛ A cowboy said to the greenhorn rider, "Hey, you're putting the saddle on backward!"

The rider replied, "You think you're so smart. You don't even know which way I'm going!"

☛ A little boy who had spent a week at a dude ranch camp told his mother excitedly, "Mom, I even saw a man who makes horses."

"Patrick, are you sure?" asked his mother.

"Yes," he replied. "He had a horse nearly finished when I saw him, and he was just nailing on the feet."

☛ A couple of polished city salesmen stopped off in a farm yard. While looking around for the farmer, they noticed a small calf that had somehow gotten its tail caught in an open knothole in the barn door.

"I can't figure out how that calf ever got through that little hole," said one salesman.

"Well, what puzzles me," said the other, "is that if he could get that far, why can't he get the rest of the way through?"

☛ A visiting group of Chicago business executives came to northern Wisconsin for a weekend of camping. They spent the day fighting off blood-sucking mosquitoes and were preparing to go to their tents for the night when the fireflies showed up.

"For heaven's sake," cried one tenderfoot, "let's get out of here. They're coming back with lanterns!"

☛ As a city tourist was driving down a country road, a huge pig ran in front of the car and was killed. The farmer saw the accident and vigorously protested his loss.

The driver was very apologetic and explained that he would replace the animal. The farmer sized up the motorist and said, "You flatter yourself."

☛ Young Johnny, visiting a farm for the first time, was awed by everything he saw. He was especially intrigued by the lightning rods on the roof of the barn.

"Golly," he gasped, "the cows even have TV!"

☛ Kate just got back to the city after spending the last week at her uncle's dairy farm and invited her boyfriend, Jim, over for dinner.

When offered some fresh milk that Kate had brought back, Jim asked, "Does your uncle keep his cows on pasture?"

"Yes, of course," Kate replied. "Why do you ask?"

"Because I only drink pasteurized milk," he said.

☛ A farmer was explaining to a city woman what a menace insects are to farm products—how corn borers destroy corn and potato bugs can ruin potato crops.

The woman listened attentively, then exclaimed, "And the poor dairy people...how the butterflies must bother them!"

☞ A farm woman was showing her city cousin around the farm. "And if you treat a cow with affection," she explained, "it will give more milk."

"Big deal," her city cousin replied. "So will the milkman."

☞ On a school field trip to the farm, a city boy spent his very first day out in the country. Everything he saw on the farm was new and wondrous.

Toward the sunset of the day, he stood intently watching the farmer's wife plucking a chicken. After a bit, his curiosity grew too great and he asked gravely, "Do you take their clothes off every night, lady?"

☞ A tourist spending the night in a small town joined several townspeople sitting on the front porch of the general store. After several futile attempts to start a conversation, he finally asked, "Is there a law against talking in this town?"

"No law against it," answered one of the men. "But there's an understanding no one's to speak unless he is sure to improve on the silence."

☞ The farm boy said to the visiting city girl, "This is a tobacco plant in full flower."

The city girl asked, "And how long will it be before the cigarettes are ripe?"

☞ One day, a city man was tired of "life in the fast lane" and decided to move his family to a more rural area. There was only one concern—he had to have a wooded lot out back.

He arrived in the country late at night, and bought a house from a fast-selling real estate agent without seeing the house. The whole family moved into the house that same night.

The next morning when he got up, he found out he couldn't see anything but trees—and more trees. He ambled over to his neighbor's lot complaining that he wanted a wooded lot but this was too much.

"Must have bought your house from the same real estate agent we got ours from," the neighbors told him. "Our lot was just like yours, but we rented a chainsaw in town. You can cut up to five cords of wood a day with those saws."

He went into town, rented a saw and went to work. All day long he toiled and sweated, but at the end of the day he only had cut one cord. Thinking that maybe he wasn't used to the gadget, he tried again the next day, working even harder. At the end of the second day, he'd only cut 3/4 of a cord.

He went back to the hardware dealer and told him of the results. "Must be something wrong with the saw, let me see," the hardware man said as he pulled the rope and the motor hummed to life.

The man looked at the hardware man in surprise, stepped back in fright and said, "What in the hell is that noise?"

☞ A city girl told the farmer, "I found a horseshoe this morning."

"Do you know what that means?"

"Yes," the young girl said, "some poor horse is walking around in his stocking feet."

☞ An Englishman recently bought a country home in the United States. He noticed flying insects in his closet and after telling the drug store clerk his problems, he was sold a box of mothballs.

Two days later he bought another box. In another two days, he was back for still another box.

The clerk finally asked, "What in the world are you doing with all those mothballs?"

"Well, gov'ner," replied the Englishman, "you just can't hit the little blighters every time."

☞ A visitor to a very small town wanted to know if there was a movie house or any other entertainment in town.

"No," said the old-timer, "but come on over to the diner. We've got a freshman home from college."

Chapter 6

A Visit To The Big City

"New York now leads the world's cities in the number of people around whom you shouldn't make a sudden move."

—*David Letterman*

☛ A midwestern farmer on his first trip to New York managed to hit all the bars in Times Square before he stumbled down a stairway leading to the subway.

Emerging a half-hour later, he met a friend who had been searching for him. "Where in the world have you been?" his friend demanded.

"Down in some guy's cellar," the man replied with glassy eyes. "And boy, has he got a set of trains."

☛ A farmer and his wife drove to the big city one weekend to see the touring orchestra. The couple recognized all the musical instruments except the slide trombone. The husband watched the player for quite some time, then said to a wife, "There's a trick to it. He ain't really swallowing it."

☛ An old backwoodsman drove to the city to have his watch repaired. When the jeweler took the watch apart, a dried bug fell out.

"No wonder it ain't runnin'," the old man grunted. "The engineer's dead."

☛ Farmer Bert was on his first visit to the city and was fascinated by the asphalt streets. Scraping his feet on the hard black surface and in deep contemplation, he remarked, "Sure can't blame them a bit for building a town here. This ground is much too hard to plow anyhow."

☛ A farm boy was visiting his cousin in the city and had to listen to the city boy's bragging for hours. "My dad is an Elk, a Lion, a Moose and an Eagle," the city boy boasted.

The farm boy said, "What does it cost to see him?"

☛ A young man in the country wrote to his uncle in the city to inquire about moving there. "Can I live a Christian life in the city for $15 a week?" he wrote.

His uncle wrote back, "That's the only thing you can do."

☛ An old hillbilly and his wife decided to spend some time in the city. Since they had never stayed overnight in a hotel before, they decided on the most expensive in the city.

A television set was turned on when they entered, so they sat down and enjoyed the show for a while.

Then the old man became angry and shouted to his wife, "Ma, tell those show people to get away from our window so I can undress and go to bed."

☛ Old Jerry retired from the farm and came to the city to get a job as a janitor at a girl's boarding school. He was entrusted with a pass key to every room in the building.

A week later, the dean ran into him and asked, "Why didn't you come around on Saturday for your wages?"

Jerry was surprised. "What?" he asked. "Do I get wages, too?"

☛ A backwoodsman mountaineer was in town and saw a mirror in a shop. As he looked into it, he said, "Well, if ain't my old dad. I never knew he had his picture shot."

He took the mirror home and hid it in the attic but his suspicious wife was watching secretly. That night she slipped up to the attic and found the mirror. "Mmmmm," she said, looking into it, "so that's the old hag he's been chasin'!"

☛ A family from rural Oklahoma took a vacation and along the way, stopped at a hotel for the first time. As they settled in their room, they noticed two large silver elevator doors at the end of the hall.

"Daddy, what are those?" the farm boy asked, pointing to the doors.

"Darned if I know," the father answered.

Just then, a bent-over, elderly woman pushed a button and the door came open and the woman entered. The numbers above the door went up 2-3-4 and then came down again. The doors flew open and out stepped a gorgeous, shapely blonde.

The farmer grabbed his son and pushed him along toward the room. "Go get your ma, son," he said, excited. "I want to run her through this thing one time before we leave."

☞ A retired farmer and his wife moved into their new home in the city. "Pa, it's time you got up and started the fire," his wife bellowed.

"Not me!" he exclaimed. "We might as well start now getting used to all the city conveniences. Call the fire department!"

☞ A farmer visiting the city for the first time came upon a sign that read: "Smith Manufacturing Company."

He thought to himself, "Well, I always knew a lot of Smiths, but I never knew where they came from."

☞ A hillbilly edged up to the ticket window of the local railroad station. "Mister," he said, "I aim to go to the city to fiddle for a band. Do you reckon you could fix me up a ticket to get there?"

"Certainly," the ticket agent said. "I can flag down the special for you—but where's your suitcase?"

"Suitcase?" asked the puzzled mountain man. "What's that fer?"

The ticket agent replied: "To put your clothes in."

"What?" cried the hillbilly, "and me ride the train naked?"

☞ A farmer returned from his first visit to New York City and met an old friend.

"Did you have a good time, Hiram?" the friend asked.

"Oh, boy, did I!" he exclaimed. "I walked down Fifth Avenue and all the girls in the windows flirted with me!"

His friend informed him, "Those weren't girls, Hiram—those were dummies."

"They weren't so dumb," Hiram said, "they all had on mink coats."

☞ When the old African headhunter caught a glimpse of a TV set for the first time, he said to his friend, "It's a wonderful machine where they can shrink the whole body."

☛ A mountaineer was driving with his wife to the city in their old truck when he saw a motorcycle buzzing alongside him. He stopped the truck, pulled his rifle out from under the seat, aimed, and shot.

"Did you get that varmint?" his half-asleep wife asked.

"Hit it, but didn't kill it," he said. "I can still hear it growlin'—but I sure made it turn that poor man loose."

☛ Farmer Mark and his wife moved to a modest home in the city. His wife complained that they needed a more expensive house.

Mark was too lazy to move, so he called up the landlord and asked him to raise the rent.

☛ A farmer and his wife were boarding their first flight and were a bit nervous. Prior to takeoff, a flight attendant walked back through the aisles handing tiny travel kits to passengers. When she reached the farm couple she handed them a pack of bubble gum. "Here," she said, "this will keep your ears from popping at high altitudes."

As the couple departed the plane, the farmer called the flight attendant aside and said, "Thanks for the gum—but how do we get this darn stuff out of our ears?"

☛ A farm boy was visiting the city and he and his cousin were trying to outdo each other. "Did you know a grasshopper can jump a distance that is more than 100 times its own length?" the farm boy asked.

His city cousin replied, "No, but I've seen a 1/10-ounce wasp lift a 250-pound man three feet off the ground!"

☛ A hillbilly took his wife and family down to the college observatory. As they watched a man peering through a telescope, a star suddenly fell.

"Good shot!" the hillbilly yelled.

☛ A gawky farm teenager came to New York with his girlfriend and took her to a nearby amusement park. They had heard about the Tunnel of Love and were anxious to try it out. But when they got home, he expressed disappointment.

"Shucks," the boy told his friends, "it was dark, damp and uncomfortable. Besides, we got soaking wet."

"How come?" asked a friend. "Did the boat leak?"

The kid looked amazed, "There's a boat?"

Just Farmin' On

*"The American farmer
prefers getting bent from
hard work rather than getting
crooked from trying to avoid it."*

Chapter 7

Down On Their Luck

*"A farmer is always
going to be rich next year."*
—Philemon

☞ A farmer wandered into a federal building and asked, "Is this the headquarters for the war against poverty?"
"Yes, it is," replied the secretary.
"Good," the farmer said. "I've come to surrender."

☞ An old farmer bought two hammers at a general store and shortly returned to buy four more. He came back later to buy eight hammers and then returned again to buy 16. Finally, the merchant asked him what he was doing with all the hammers.
"I'm selling them," the farmer replied.
"What are you getting for them?" the storekeeper asked.
"A dollar and a quarter."
"Man, you can't make any money that way," the merchant protested. "You're paying a dollar and a half for them."
"Well," the farmer said, "it still beats farming."

☞ A working definition of a farmer? A man who wears out two pairs of overalls before making enough money to buy one pair.

☞ A tribe in Africa was having a terrible time with its food supply because of bad crops. The worried natives went to their chief with the crisis.
The chief said, "What we'll do is send a telegram to the Russians telling them that we are having agricultural problems and we need their assistance. They will send us seeds and tractors and 100 young technicians to help us.
"Then we'll send a telegram to the United States telling them the Russians are sending us seeds, tractors and 100

technicians. This will make the U.S. send us seeds, tractors and 200 technicians."

Then the chief added, "And when all the technicians arrive, we'll eat them."

☛ A farmer was talking taxes with a business acquaintance at a meeting. "We're a non-profit organization," he said. "We didn't mean to be, but we are."

☛ A farm expert is someone who is called in at the last minute to share the blame.

☛ Two farmers were discussing their status in life. "I started out on the theory that the world had an opening for me," one man said.

"And have you found it?" the other farmer asked.

"Well, yes," replied the first. "I'm in the hole now."

☛ Two farmers were talking at the local pub. "What time is it by your watch?" the first farmer asked.

"Quarter to," Ronald answered.

"Quarter to what?"

"I can't tell," Ronald said. "Times got so bad I had to lay off one of the hands."

☛ After selling his crops for a great profit, a farmer stopped at a small town diner and started a discussion with a stranger next to him. "Success in agriculture," he bragged, "is getting in your pickup truck and being able to drive across your land all day long."

The other man, who also happened to be a farmer, said, "Yeah, I know. I used to have an old broken-down truck like that myself."

☛ The Yankee farmer, after seven years of effort on his stony New England farm, announced to all: "Anyhow, I'm holding my own. I didn't have nothin' when I came here and I ain't got nothin' now."

☛ A farmer was reading a magazine that proclaimed, "Half of the world is said to be engaged in agriculture." The farmer said to himself, "So that's how the other half lives."

☛ A city merchant, a school teacher and a farmer were discussing what they would do if they awoke one morning to discover they were millionaires.

The merchant said he'd build a giant shopping center so he could double his money.

The teacher said she'd go back to college and get all the available education possible.

"I," said the farmer, "would just continue to farm until it was all spent."

☛ Everyone was shocked when the stingy old farmer bought an expensive surrealistic painting that was so modern you couldn't tell up from down.

When asked why he bought it, he replied, "Best picture I've ever seen of the farm situation."

☛ A young man was visiting the large ranch owned by his girlfriend's father for the first time. He asked her father, "Does this spread go all the way to the group of trees where those cattle are resting?"

"Yep," answered the rancher, "and it goes past those oil wells over there and to the other side of that wheat field."

By this time, the young man's eyes were glazed over with dollar signs.

"There's just one place it doesn't go," the farmer said. "It doesn't go to my daughter."

☛ What are the three most beautiful words in the English language?

To a young woman they might be, "I love you."

To a married man, "Home sweet home" is a good guess.

But to the farmer, there's no question—"Enclosed find check!"

☛ A farm magazine editor was explaining the advantages of being a subscriber. While he gave his sales pitch to a farmer, he said, "Why, we carry several articles every month telling you how to do a better job of farming."

"Ain't interested," the farmer told him. "I'm not farming half as well as I know how now."

☛ The only difference between the gambling casino and a farmer is that the casino is always guaranteed a 20 percent take!

☞ A farmer and his little boy were talking after a very bad crop year. "Dad," the boy asked, "what was your goal in life when you were little?"

The farmer said, "To wear long pants, son, and I've got my wish. If there's anybody who wears his pants longer than I do, I'd like to see him."

☞ A Kansas farmer who had been hit by the severe drought went into a small bank to see about getting a farm loan. "I think I might be able to do it," said the banker, "but maybe we'd better drive out and appraise your property."

"No need to trouble yourself," the farmer said as he looked out the window and saw a vast dust cloud rolling up over the horizon. "Here it comes now."

☞ A relief worker had driven four miles to see an apparently deserving farmer. Before she approved him for relief, however, she checked on a rumor that was going around the welfare office.

"We were told," she said, "that you have been driving a car. Do you own one? You know we aren't giving help to people who are able to own cars."

The farmer promptly replied, "No, lady, I sometimes drive a car, but it isn't mine. It's loaned to me."

But the worker persisted. "But they say that your daughter drives a car to high school almost every day."

"Well," the farmer confessed, "it's like this about that car. It belongs to my brother-in-law's sister and sometimes she lets us drive it. My daughter hasn't any other way to get to school, so she's been letting her use it."

That explanation seemed satisfactory and the worker left the food and home supplies.

As she disappeared in the distance, the farmer turned to his neighbor and said, "That old fool never will figure out that my brother-in-law's sister is my wife."

☞ Three farmers were hunting together in Canada and each of them bagged huge, trophy-sized moose. Their celebrating was darkened by only one important concern: Was their small plane strong enough to carry the hunting party and all three animals?

The farmers, buoyed by optimism, decided that it was. They took off, headed for home—and the plane crashed.

The plane was a wreck, the moose were lost, but somehow the farmers all survived. "Oh well," one farmer said to another, "at least we made it farther than we did last year."

☛ There seems to be two schools of thought on what qualifications make a master farmer. One group contends that a master farmer is one who can pay his taxes without borrowing money.

The other group believes a master farmer is one who is able to borrow the money to pay taxes.

☛ Some say farming is like raising pigeons—you've got to keep your eye on the overhead.

☛ Years of living through disastrous floods on his small bottomland farm had made Ben proud of taking trouble without much fussing.

One year, however, the river not only flooded out his cornfield as usual, but chased Ben and his wife clear out of the house. When they returned to clean up the mess, it was even worse—during the flood, the river changed course and had wiped out their entire farm.

After Ben had stared for several minutes at the water where his house and barn had been, his wife began to fear that this final blow might have unhinged his mind. "S-say something, Pa," she said timidly.

But Ben was equal to the occasion. He took one look, rubbed his jaw and spat into the river. "Thorough," he said, "ain't it?"

☛ As her husband walked in the door and threw his cap on the table, the farm wife said, "You look tired, dear. Did you have a bad day?"

"I'll say," he responded. "I took an aptitude test in town, and believe me, it's a good thing I own the farm."

☛ Minnesota store owners say a tourist-farmer from Iowa was an easy one to spot. According to them, he wore bib overalls, carried a $20 bill and never changed either for two weeks.

☛ An Oklahoma rancher had no success with anything in his life. He made no money, his kids all turned out poorly, his wife ran off and left him, and he developed a bad case of rheumatism in his older age.

But his luck finally changed—when they dug his grave, they struck oil.

☞ Why do they bury a farmer only three feet deep now? So he can keep his hand out.

☞ Farmer Giles dropped into the inn on his way back from market. "How'd the wheat crop turn out, Mr. Giles?" the innkeeper asked.

"Oh," replied Giles, "de ducks got my crop."

"Ducks? Do you mean wild ducks?"

"No," replied the farmer, shaking his head sadly, "not wild ducks—de ducks. I sent a load of wheat to the city and I've just got my returns. They sold the wheat all right, but they de ducks the insurance, they de ducks the handling charges they de ducks their commission. De ducks got all the money."

☞ Not as many farmers have lost faith in America as you might think. An awful lot of them are signing up for 30-year mortgages.

☞ "I've just discovered oil on our property," the farmer said as he walked into the house.

"Wonderful!" exclaimed his wife. "Now we can get a new car!"

"We'd better get the old one fixed," he replied. "That's where the oil is coming from."

☞ Two farmers, who hadn't seen each other since their poverty-stricken childhood, met at the fair. One of the men smugly began to remind the other about his humble origin.

"Remember when you only had one pair of shoes to your name, Harry?" the first one asked, laughing.

"I sure do," the second man replied. "You asked me what they were used for."

☞ A daughter approached her dad for help. "What do you want now, Thelma?" her dad said. "Haven't I just set your husband up in farming?"

"Yes, I know, Dad," the daughter said. "But now he wants you to buy him out."

☞ Definitions for today's farmer:

Recession: When your neighbor loses his farm.

Depression: When you lose your farm.

Panic: When your wife loses her job in town.

☛ It had been a rough row for George. During frequent trips to town to get machinery repairs and to pay off his bank loan, he often stopped by the mental hospital and watched one patient out in the hospital's yard going through the motions of pitching a baseball.

A friend saw George watching one day and later asked him why he sat out there by the hospital.

George replied, "Well, another season like this one and I'll be catching for that fellow—and I want to be sure to know what kind of curve he throws."

Chapter 8

A Day At The Farm

"Many of our great men used to come from the farm. We don't have any of that surplus now."

☛ A kindhearted farmer came upon a young boy who had just lost a load of hay along the side of the road, and suggested that the boy come home with him and have dinner before reloading the wagon.

"I don't think my father would like that," said the boy, but the farmer persisted until the boy finally agreed. After eating a hearty dinner and relaxing a bit, the farmer drove the boy back to the scene of the accident and started to help him put the hay back on the wagon.

"By the way," the farmer said. "You're awfully young to be pulling this hay yourself. Where's your dad?"

The boy answered, "He's under this hay."

☛ "So, I hear you are undertaking bees?" the farmer was asked.

"Yes," he replied. "I don't want to miss anything and I've been stung every other way there is."

☛ A tourist stopped by the roadside to have his picnic lunch and look over the countryside. He struck up a conversation with a farmer who was working near the fence.

"You have a beautiful farm here," the tourist said. "What do you raise?"

"A bit of this and that. Corn, beans, pigs and cattle."

"It must keep you busy," the tourist said. "What time do you go to work everyday?"

"I don't go to work," the farmer said, "I wake up every morning surrounded by it."

☛ What have you got when you put eight farmers in the basement? A whine cellar.

☞ A farm is a hunk of land on which, if you get up early enough on mornings and work late enough at night, you'll make a fortune if you strike oil.

☞ A backwoods farmer was offered 10 times what his property was worth after the railroad officials explained to him that a proposed cut-off would run right through the spot where his barn stood.

The farmer astounded everybody by turning down the money.

He defended himself to his outraged wife by shouting, "No, siree. You won't catch me having to run out to that barn day and night to open and shut the door every time they want to send a train through."

☞ A free-advice-seeking woman asked a farmer what would be good to plant in a spot that gets very little rain due to overhanging leaves, has too much late afternoon sun, has clay soil and is on a rocky ledge.

"Lady," he answered, "how about a nice flagpole?"

☞ Asked by a reporter where he'd like to be if a nuclear bomb went off, a farmer replied, "Somewhere so I could say, 'What was that?'"

☞ Farmer Otis acquired a team of mules and decided a barn should be built to protect them against the elements. Not much of a construction man, he finally settled for a pole shed with a dirt floor.

When it was completed, he led the mules into the shed and thought he had, indeed, solved the housing problem. But a couple of weeks later, he discovered the ears on his mules were showing signs of wear from the ceiling beams.

One day a neighbor stopped by and found the farmer setting up a series of jacks to raise the structure and place it up on some blocks.

"Otis," the neighbor asked, "why don't you just dig out a little of the soft dirt?"

"What do you mean?" Otis asked his neighbor. "It isn't too short for the mule's legs—it's too short for the mule's ears."

☞ A farmer was quietly eating lunch at a roadside diner when three bikers began taunting him. They spilled his food, pushed him off his stool and called him names. The farmer said nothing as he got up off the floor, paid his bill and left.

One of the hoodlums, disappointed that they hadn't provoked some kind of fight, said to the waitress, "Boy, he sure wasn't much of a man, was he?"

"Not much of a driver, either," she responded as she looked out the window. "He just backed over three motorcycles."

☞ A tenderfoot from the city moved out to the country to farm and asked an old Indian farmer when cotton should be planted.

The Indian answered, "Get up in the morning and sit on the ground. If it is cold, don't plant."

☞ It was late September when two motorists stopped along a rural highway to eat lunch. The crows were especially noisy, prompting a discussion as to whether the varying "caws" emitting from the birds constituted a language. Over a stone wall a farmer was doing some planting and they asked his opinion.

"Sure, they talk," said the farmer. "Just had a talk with one."

"You mean to say you talk 'crow talk' with them?"

"Nope," the farmer said. "These crows speak English. He flapped down onto a branch on that elm over there and looked down at me and asked, 'Cawn?' I looked up at him and said, 'Nope, beans.'

'Aw,' he said, and off he flew."

☞ "Jim Bob," ordered the farmer, "All clocks in the house have run down. Hitch up and ride down to the junction to see what time it is."

Jim Bob replied, "But I ain't got a watch. Will you lend me one?"

"Watch? Watch? What do you want a watch for?" the farmer questioned. "Just write it down on a piece of paper."

☞ Farmers are a pessimistic bunch. If it rains, they start looking for a flood. If it's dry, they predict a drought.

One year, though, everything was perfect. Weather was ideal, crops were abundant, and prices at the market were high. One old farmer, who always seemed to find something to gripe about, won a prize for the most bushels of corn. A local merchant congratulated the old pessimist.

"Great work, John," he said. "225 bushels of corn to the acre. That's marvelous!"

"I don't know," the farmer said, shaking his head sadly. "It's awful hard on the soil."

☞ A man walked over to the garden fence and was shocked at what he saw. He said to his neighboring farmer, "It's useless sowing seeds two feet deep."

"I know," the farmer replied, "but it really annoys the birds."

☞ As the county agent sat relaxing with his feet up on the desk, he was startled by a fellow who came into the office carrying a sack of dirt and asking where he could get his soil tested.

"How did you take your samples?" the agent asked.

The farmer replied, "Well, I'll tell you. I waited for a rainy day, drove the tractor all over the farm, and then just cleaned off the tires."

☞ A government official instructed the old farmer to collect his stock of every description and have them branded.

"I suppose that's all right," sighed the farmer, scratching his head. "But honest, mister, I'm going to have a terrible time with them bees."

☞ Patrick was new working as a farm hand and his first attempt was anything but successful.

"Look here!" said the farmer, "that kind of thing won't do. Corn that grows in a row as crooked as that will be dizzy. Fix your eyes on something across the field and plow straight toward it. Look, that cow there by the gate is right opposite us. Aim at her and you'll do pretty well."

"All right, sir," Patrick said. Just then, the farmer was called away to the barn. Fifteen minutes later he returned, and was horrified to see that the plow had been wandering in a zigzag course all over the field.

"Hold on there!" he shouted. "Hold on! What are you doing?"

A shocked Patrick said, "I did what you told me. I plowed straight for the cow, but the darn creature wouldn't keep still."

Chapter 9

Going To Seed

"There is no better demonstration of faith than a man planting seed in a field."

☞ "Your methods are a century behind the times," the pompous government expert said to the veteran farmer. "I'd be surprised if you got a bushel of wheat to the acre out of that field."

"So would I," replied the farmer. "That's barley."

☞ A man was walking through his neighbor's farm and yelled, "Cecil, why are you jumping up and down in the potato patch?"

"Because," Cecil replied, "I'm trying to raise mashed potatoes."

☞ A city visitor asked the farmer if a certain fertilizer stimulated a plant's growth.

"I've never been able to figure out whether the stuff actually stimulates the plants," replied the farmer, "or if it's so repulsive they try to grow away from it."

☞ As the farmers toured the corn research plots, the experiment station agronomist said, "What we're breeding for is a dwarf corn with short stalks and smaller ears closer to the ground."

When the agronomist paused, a sand-hill farmer blurted out, "Shucks, professor, you don't have to breed for that. I've been growing corn like that all my life."

☞ During the agricultural science course at the university, a professor spoke of a miracle plant that scientists are trying to develop. This plant grows in any kind of weather, is resistant to insects and requires no fertilizer or care.

A voice from the back of the lecture hall said, "Professor, it's called a weed."

☞ A gentleman farmer is one who tips his hat every time he passes a good looking tomato.

☞ There was an old farmer named Elton who was an incurable grumbler. One fall he had the best apple crop for miles around. One of his neighbors thought it was a good time to congratulate him.

"Well, Elton, you ought to be happy now. Yours is the finest apple crop ever raised in these parts."

But the grumbler didn't even smile as he groaned. "Well, I suppose it will do, but now where are the rotten ones for the hogs?"

☞ A depressed man went to the doctor and was given this advice: "Forget your troubles and bury yourself in your work."

Astonished, he replied, "But, Doc, I work in a fertilizer factory."

☞ Two Alaskan farmers were constantly arguing over who grew the largest crops. One morning the first told his son, "Jimmy, go over to Mr. Pendleton's house and borrow his crosscut saw. Tell him I want to cut a watermelon."

Jimmy was back in a hurry. "Can't have it today," he told his dad. "Mr. Pendleton says his wife isn't through slicing cucumbers."

☞ A new county agent, visiting a mountain farm for the first time asked, "Do you people have any trouble with insects in your corn?"

"We sure do," the farmer replied, "but we just fish 'em out and drink it anyhow."

☞ Two farmers were discussing their crops over the past year. "We never did go back to dig our potatoes," Arnold said.

"You didn't? Why not?" his friend asked.

"The seed catalog said to plant them in hills," Arnold said, "and the closest hills are over 50 miles from here."

☛ Out of curiosity, a farmer had grown a crop of flax, and had a tablecloth made out of the linen. Sometime later he bragged about it to a woman at his wife's dinner party. "I grew this tablecloth myself," he boasted.

"Did you really?" she exclaimed. "How on earth did you manage it?

It was obvious that she had no idea as to how tablecloths came into being, so the farmer lowered his voice mysteriously. "If you promise to keep the secret, I'll tell you."

The guest promised. "Well," proceeded the farmer, "I planted a napkin."

☛ It has been said that telling secrets on the farm is dangerous—the potatoes have eyes, corn has ears and the beans-talk.

☛ An old Hoosier farmer, declining assistance after a severe Wabash River flood, remarked, "But you might tell them farmers upriver to use a bit more fertilizer. This silt we get now ain't half as rich as it used to be."

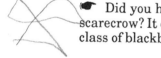 ☛ Did you hear about the farmer who put a tuxedo on his scarecrow? It didn't protect the corn, but it attracted a better class of blackbirds!

☛ At the ladies' gardening club, an amateur asked "When the seeds come up, how can you tell the plants from the weeds?"

"Pull them up," declared Rosie, "the ones that come up again are the weeds."

☛ An untimely frost completed the problems created earlier by the insect enemies of Mr. Perkins' potatoes. The tops of the plants, which had served as food for the pests, were entirely destroyed, and with them, Mr. Perkins' hope of a crop. He was not selfish, however, and could think of others in his hour of adversity. In the afternoon he was accosted at the post office by a friend.

"Hello, Perkins! How's everything up to the corners?"

"Trouble enough, Williamson, trouble enough!" was the gloomy response. "Ten million potato-bugs, and nothing for 'em to eat!"

☛ During the farm picnic, a snooty old lady from town went around sniffing and asking, "What's that terrible odor I smell?"

The farmer said, "Lady, that's fertilizer."

The old lady was astonished and said, "Oh, for land's sake!"

The farmer laughed and said, "That's right, ma'am."

☛ Even for crops, the inevitable question always comes up. The baby ear of corn said, "Mama, where did I come from?"

The mother ear of corn quickly replied, "Hush, dear—the stalk brought you."

☛ Larry, who farmed very hilly land, was talking to his neighbor when he was asked about his first-ever potato crop. "I haven't seen your potato digger. What are you going to do about harvesting?"

"Oh, I don't have a digger," Larry said. "Well, my land's so hilly, I'll just go to the bottom of the hill with some sacks, dig a hole in the end of each row, hold the sack, and the potatoes will just roll down the row into the sack."

☛ Just think of the crops we'd grow if the fertilizer salesman's goods were half as rich as his conversation.

☛ Lecturing a group of wheat farmers on the latest contributions of chemistry to agriculture, the young scientist declared, "The time is coming when a farmer will be able to carry all the fertilizer for an acre of ground in one pants pocket."

"Sure," grunted the old farmer, "and all the crop in the other."

☛ The young farmer was telling his city aunt that the best thing to use for flowers is manure. The aunt scolded, "Please, Henry, around here we call it fertilizer."

Henry's answer shocked her. "Easy, Aunt Hazel," he said, "it took us three years back home to get them to say manure."

A Day With The Animals

"Man is the only animal that laughs, but when you look at some farmers, it's hard to understand how the animals keep from laughing."

Chapter 10

From the
Horse's Mouth...

"Horse sense is that quality possessed by horses that keeps them from acting like people."

☛ A sickly-looking horse was being offered to the highest bidder at the county auction. An old farmer watched as a young man in riding britches earnestly bid for the animal.

When the young man came away with the old horse, the farmer turned to him and said, "Tell me, what on earth are you going to do with that nag?"

"Oh," replied the cocky young sportsman, "I'm going to race her."

After taking a second look at the animal, the farmer said, "Well, son, you'll win."

☛ A farmer drove through town pulling a hay wagon with only one mule. As the farmer yelled to his one mule, "Giddap Pete! Giddap Barney! Giddap Johnny! Giddap Ralph!" a crowd of people gathered to see what was going on.

Finally, a stranger asked, "How many names does that mule have?"

"His name's Pete," said the farmer. "But he don't know his own strength so I put blinders on him and yell a lot of names so he thinks a lot of other mules are helping him."

☛ A wealthy but not too wise suburbanite bought two horses from a rancher. He never seemed able to tell them apart so he cut the tail off one horse. To his dismay, the tail grew back. Determined, he cut off the mane of the other horse. But this didn't work either since it also grew back. He still was unable to tell them apart.

Finally, in desperation, he measured them and discovered that the white horse was two inches taller than the black horse.

☛ The farmer dropped the load in the bathtub and said, "That'll be another $10 for porter charges." The man gave the farmer the money and as he walked out the door, the perplexed farmer turned and asked, "But why in the world do you want a dead horse in the bathtub?"

"You have to know my brother-in-law," the man answered. "He and his wife come over every weekend to play bridge. He thinks he so darned smart. He asks things like, 'George, how many trees are there in the national forests?' How do I know? Then he rattles off, '10,873,793,172.' His wife beams on account of what a smart man she married. My wife gives me a dingy look that says, 'You dumb cluck!'

"Then he asks, 'George, how many stars are there in the Milky Way constellation?' Of course I don't know, so we get a repeat of his act. His wife smirks and my wife scowls."

"So why the dead horse?" the farmer asked.

The man answered, "Well, this Saturday night will be different. After he mouths off a few times and has a couple of beers, he'll have to go to the bathroom. He'll come out running and yelling, 'George, what in the world do you have in the bathtub?'

"That's when I get even, finally! I'll smile and say, 'You dingbat, that's a dead horse.'"

☛ A midwestern farmer, in town for his routine Saturday trip to the feed store, happened to run into the local veterinarian.

"Got a problem for you, Doc," the farmer said. "I've got a horse that walks normal sometimes and then other times, he limps badly. What can I do with him?"

The vet scratched his head and said, "Well, the next time he walks normal, sell him!"

☛ A farmer with a lazy, sorry-looking mule envied his neighbor, who owned a tall, strong mule named Buckshot. The neighbor bragged that whenever he needed to get plenty of work out of Buckshot, all he needed to do was talk to him.

Finally, the farmer bought Buckshot from his neighbor, even though the price for the mule was outrageously expensive. However, no amount of talking could get the animal to do any work.

After days of talking, the disgusted farmer confronted his neighbor about the mule. The neighbor picked up a two-by-four and hit the mule right between the eyes, stunning him.

"I forgot to tell you," the neighbor said, "first, you've got to get his attention."

☛ Two horse traders were arguing over the terms of a swap. "Tell me," said one, "has anyone ever questioned my honesty?"

"Well, no," was the reply. "But it's never been mentioned either."

☛ A man was walking down a country road when he saw a horse standing quietly near a fence. He walked over and patted the horse on the head and said, "I wish I owned a beautiful horse like you."

"Why, thank you very much," the horse said, surprising the man. "It isn't often that I get a compliment like that."

The man was amazed. "You're talking!" he said. "A talking horse!"

"That's right," the horse said with pride. "And that's not all. Would you believe that I once won the Kentucky Derby?"

"That certainly is something," the man said. Just then, he saw the horse's owner.

"Your horse just talked to me," the man said.

"Sure, sure," the owner said. "And I'll bet he gave you that nonsense about the Kentucky Derby, too."

Chapter 11

With A Moo-Moo Here...

"The reason the cow jumped over the moon was because there was a short circuit in the milking machine."

☞ Two cows were grazing along the highway when a tank truck of milk approached. On the side of the vehicle was printed: "Pasteurized, homogenized, standardized, with vitamin A added."

As the great white truck rumbled by, one cow turned to the other and said, "Makes you feel sort of inadequate, doesn't it?"

☞ A farmer was standing by a bull when a man came by and asked, "Does your bull charge?"

The farmer answered politely, "No, sir, my bull does not charge."

So the man walked by the bull and the bull snorted and charged him. Out of breath from running, he screamed to the farmer, "I thought you said your bull doesn't charge!"

The farmer said, "Sir, this is not my bull."

☞ During his routine inspection, the DHIA tester asked a farmer, "Why do you call this cow 'Lightning?'"

"We used to call her Daisy until we tried to milk her," said the farmer as he rubbed his swollen knee. "Then we changed it to Lightning because she never strikes the same place twice."

☞ As the schoolmarm was correcting her weekly quizzes, she came across Ralph's peculiar answer to the question, "What is a cow?"

Ralph wrote, "She's a creature with four stander-uppers, four puller-downers, two hookers, two lookers and one switcher."

☛ If you've ever wanted a definition of an ultimatum, consider the farmer, pail in hand, who looked at his cow and said, "Well, Bossy, what'll it be? Milk or hamburger?"

☛ A frantic hiker spotted a farmer out by the barn and ran over to him. "I can catch the 6:15 train," explained the hiker, "if you'll let me cut across your field."

"Go right ahead," said the farmer, "but you'll be able to catch the 5:45 if my bull spots you."

☛ While Mary, a young farm girl was milking a cow, a bull tore across the meadow toward her. The girl did not stir, but continued her diligent milking.

Farm hands, who saw the bull charging and had run to safety, saw to their amazement that the giant bull stopped dead in its tracks within a few yards of the girl, turned around and sadly walked away. "Gosh, weren't you afraid?" everyone asked her.

Mary looked up from her milking and said, "Certainly not. I happen to know this cow is his mother-in-law."

☛ A Quaker became angry at a cow for kicking a full bucket of milk all over his Sunday clothes.

"Thou knowest that because of my religion I cannot punish thee," he said, raising his voice. "But if you doest this deed again, I will sellest thee to a Baptist minister and he will kick thee so that thou can never kick again."

☛ Young Willie walked up to his dad who was working in the barn and asked, "Do you know how to stop a cow from having calves?"

"No, I suspect I don't," the farmer replied.

A giggling Willie said, "You feed her Apple Jacks—it keeps the bullies away."

☛ Roscoe always maintained his success in dairy farming was due to outsmarting the animals he raised. His theory was proved to a neighbor one day when he found Roscoe putting forkfuls of hay along the shed roof.

"What's the idea, Roscoe?" he called as he climbed out of the car.

"Oh, like I always say," Roscoe began philosophically, "you have to be smarter than the animals."

"So?" his neighbor asked impatiently.

"Well, as you know, I had a bad crop this year," he said. "If I put it in the manger, the cows won't eat it. But if I put it up here where they can just reach it, they think they're stealing it and they'll eat every bit."

☞ Two farm kids were swinging on the park swings. "Hey Michael," said little Penny, "what walks in the field during the day and sits in the icebox at night?"

Michael answered, "I dunno."

"Milk," Penny giggled.

☞ A tight-wad farmer was approached by a stranger one day and asked, "How much is that prize Jersey heifer of yours worth?"

The farmer scratched his chin for a moment and then asked, "Are you the tax assessor or has she been killed by a truck?"

☞ A farmer was checking out the dairy cows at the county auction. After spotting one he was interested in, he asked the auctioneer, "Does she give lots of milk?"

"No, I can't say she gives a lot of milk, but I can tell you this," said the auctioneer. "She's a kind, gentle, good-natured old cow and if she's got any milk she'll give it to you."

☞ Unable to get experienced help, a farmer was forced to hire a man unfamiliar with farm chores. One day, he walked into the milking parlor to find the hired hand forcing old Bessy to drink a pail of milk.

"Say, fellow," he said. "What's the big idea of feeding that pail of milk to the cow?"

"Well," replied the new hand, "this darn cow stepped in it and got it dirty, so I'm running it through again."

Chapter 12

Where's The Beef?

"If the bravest are the tenderest, the cow that provided our dinner was a coward."

☛ A farmer who owned three tractors was out plowing with a bull one afternoon. A neighboring farmer stopped by and asked, "Why are you plowing that way when you've got three tractors in the barn?"

The farmer said, "I'm teaching this bull a lesson—there's more to life than just making love and knocking down fences."

☛ "I'm going to send that darned bull to the packinghouse," complained a disgusted farmer to his wife. "He's almost killed me four times now."

"Oh," begged the wife, "please give him another chance."

☛ Two ranchers were discussing the problems of the recent drought. "How are things out your way?" asked the first rancher.

"Well," answered the second, "the cattle are so thin that by using carbon paper we've been branding them two at a time."

☛ A Protestant minister, a Catholic priest and a cattle rancher were in Africa on a foreign mission, going from village to village helping people with their farming problems.

The three men came to a wide but shallow river infested with man-eating crocodiles. There was no bridge, so they would have to wade across to the other side.

The Protestant minister volunteered to go first. He said, "I know I'll be saved because I am a believer in the Bible. Jesus loves me and wants me to continue to spread His word. God will stand by me and protect me as I cross the river."

The minister started to cross the river and wasn't halfway across when a giant crocodile surfaced, opened its jaws and swallowed him whole.

Next, the Catholic priest said, "I am a priest, after all. I am a man of faith and I believe God will stand by me so I can continue his good work."

The priest made it no further than halfway when the crocodile appeared, opened its jaws and devoured him.

That left the cattle rancher who said, "I am a man of the land. I help feed the world with my beef products. I know I'll be OK so I can show these villagers how to raise cattle."

To make himself a bit lighter, the rancher took off his coat, trousers and boots. All he wore was a t-shirt with some sort of slogan printed across it.

He started to wade across the river. He wasn't halfway across when a crocodile came up, opened its jaws, and was ready to swallow him when he saw the slogan on the t-shirt.

Suddenly, it closed its jaws and swam away. The beef rancher made it to the other side.

What was printed on the beef rancher's shirt? "Beef Prices Are Now $125 per Hundredweight." Not even a crocodile could swallow that!

☞ An old-time rancher had a bull who wasn't doing too well with the cows. The farmer went to the vet and got some secret medicine. Crossing his fingers, the old farmer gave it to his bull that afternoon and immediately the bull really started going to town.

Even the farmer's neighbor noticed a change in the bull. "What's in that secret medicine, anyway?" he asked.

The old farmer replied, "I don't know, but it sure tastes like peppermint."

☞ A smiling young farm boy asked his teacher, "What do you call a cow that sits on the grass all the time?"

Unable to come up with the answer, his teacher said, "I don't know, what?"

He smiled and said, "Ground beef."

☞ While on vacation, an outspoken Texan watched a famed matador in a bull ring in Mexico. The bull fight reached the stage when the fearless matador, armed only with his red cape, was taunting the bull to charge at him. He avoided the animal's sharp horns only by inches, flipping the cape to the side as the angry bull roared past.

He did this several times and finally the Texan could stand it no longer. He got to his feet and shouted, "Bud, he ain't never going to run into that sack unless you hold it still."

☛ While attending a rural art show, a city visitor stopped to look at a peculiar painting. She asked the artist next to her, "What's that supposed to be?"

The bored artist replied, "That's a picture of a cow grazing." Which prompted her reply, "Where's the grass?"

"The cow ate it," the artist said.

"Well, where's the cow then," she asked again.

"You don't think she'd be silly enough to stick around after she ate up all the grass, do you?" said the artist.

☛ Eddie wandered into the local tavern and hollered, "Hey, barkeep! What do you have for a cowboy who's just in after a two-month cattle drive?"

The bartender, who had begun to walk down to serve the man, stopped dead in his tracks and yelled back, "Industrial-strength cologne."

☛ One rancher was talking to another. "What's the name of your spread?" asked the first.

"The XWK Circle Q Bar S," replied the second.

"How many head do you have?"

"Well," the second rancher answered, "only a handful. Not many survive the branding."

☛ Two farm wives were talking about the problems their husbands were having on the farm. After one wife said her husband couldn't sleep at night, the other wife said, "Despite the cattle market, my Johnny sleeps like a baby."

"Really?" the first wife asked, a bit surprised.

"Yes," she answered. "He sleeps for two hours, wakes up and cries for 30 minutes, sleeps two hours, cries for 30 minutes..."

☛ A pair of 500-pound Angus bulls were watching as the farmer unloaded a big old 1,500-pound Charolais bull from his truck.

One of the little Angus bulls went out behind the barn and started bellowing and pawing the ground. The other Angus bull, surprised at his friend's actions, asked, "Are you crazy? You aren't going to fight him are you?"

The first Angus bull replied, "No, but I certainly don't want him to think I'm a heifer, either."

Chapter 13

When Pigs Fly...

"No man should be allowed to be President who does not understand hogs, or hasn't been around a manure pile."

—*Harry S. Truman*

☛ A tourist stopped to talk to an old hog farmer. "I see you raise hogs, almost exclusively around here," he said. "Do they pay better than corn and potatoes?"

"Well, no," drawled the farmer, "but hogs don't need no hoeing."

☛ A farmer and his friend were sitting on the porch drinking lemonade when the visitor saw a three-legged pig scamper across the farmyard. Curious, he asked the farmer what happened to the pig's missing leg. Instead of answering the question, the farmer rambled on and on about what an amazing pig it was.

"It's smarter than any dog I've ever seen," the farmer said, "and twice as smart as some humans."

"Really?"

"And that ain't all," the farmer told his friend. "Once, out in the field, that pig was sniffin' around and dug up a bag of gold coins."

"That's amazing," his friend said.

"Then there's the time the neighbor boy fell into the farm pond and the pig dove in and rescued him," the farmer said.

"All right, already, it's a remarkable pig," his friend said impatiently. "But you still haven't told me how that pig came to have a missing leg."

The farmer looked him right in the eye. "Hey," he said, "you don't eat an amazing pig like that all at once."

☛ A family of pigs had just moved into their new modern home on the farm. It was an extremely neat and clean metal enclosure with a soft floor and a fountain in the center which sprayed water so the pigs could bathe and keep clean.

"Oh, goody," said the mother pig as she looked over the new quarters. "This is just what I've always wanted—a fountain pen."

☞ Dragging his head a bit, a pig walked up to his friend, the cow, in the barnyard. "What's the matter?" the cow asked.

"I'm so unpopular on this farm," the pig said. "No one is nice to me. Look at you—people are always talking about your gentleness and your kind eyes. Sure, you give milk and cream, but I give even more. I give bacon and ham. And they even pickle my feet! Still, nobody likes me. Why is this?"

The cow thought over his friend's situation for a moment or two and said, "Well, it may be because I give while I'm still living."

☞ Farming is getting so tough that two brothers in the hog-raising business are still losing money. One steals the hogs and the other steals the feed, and they are still losing $5 a head.

☞ A frustrated hog farmer was talking to his wife as a pig darted by. "I think 'Ink' will be a good name for that little pig."

"Why?" his wife asked.

"Well," the farmer said, "because he's always running out of the pen."

☞ The hen and the pig walking together down the road passed a little restaurant advertising, "Ham and Eggs."

"Let's go in," said the hen, "and make a contribution."

"Hen," said the pig, "it's all right for you to talk about a contribution, but for me it would be a total commitment."

☞ An old farmer was moodily regarding the ravages of the flood. "Hiram, your pigs are all washed down the creek," a neighbor said sympathetically.

"How about Flaherty's pigs?" asked the farmer.

"They're gone too," said the neighbor.

"And Larsen's?" the farmer asked.

"Yep."

"Humph," the farmer exclaimed, suddenly cheering up. "Ain't as bad as I thought."

Chapter 14

Here's Looking At Ewe, Kid

"One thing is for sure—a
sheep is not a creature of the air."

—Graham Chapman,
"Monty Python's Flying Circus"

☞ Two farmers were talking at the Farm Bureau meeting. One farmer asked another what kind of farm he ran and the fellow told him he raised sheep.
"How many sheep do you have?" the curious farmer asked.
"I don't know," he said. "Every time I try to count them, I fall asleep."

☞ Two farmers were talking by the fence. "By the way, George," Charlie said, "I heard you traded for a goat."
George said, "Yeah, that's right. I got him last week."
"Where do you keep him?"
"We keep him under the bed."
"Well, what do you do about the smell?" Charlie asked.
George just shrugged his shoulders and said, "He'll just have to get used to it."

☞ The milkmaid put on her coat
And went out to milk the goat.
She tried and tried,
Then she cried,
"Oh, Nanny be still."
The goat tried and tried,
But then replied,
"I'm not Nanny, I'm Bill."

☞ A public hearing was called to order in a rural township that was having trouble protecting its sheep from western coyotes. At the hearing, a woman stood up and said, "Instead of poisoning them, why not just lasso the coyotes and castrate the males?"

After a moment, an old sheep rancher raised his hand and said, "Look, lady, those coyotes ain't breeding our sheep—they're eating them."

☛ A flock of sheep was grazing happily in the meadow. "Baa-aa-aaa," said the first sheep.

"Mooooo," said the second sheep.

The first sheep turned and said, "What do you mean, Mooooo?"

The second sheep said proudly, "I'm studying a foreign language."

☛ A farmer watched as a ram ran over a cliff. He turned to his wife and said, "Uh-oh. He didn't see the ewe turn."

☛ A small boy was wandering through a sheep pasture when he met a sheep. He sang, "Black sheep, black sheep, have you any wool?"

The sheep looked up in disgust and said, "What do you think I have, kid, nylon?"

☛ A motorist was driving in the country when suddenly his car broke down. He got out of the car and was checking the spark plugs when an old goat trotted up the road.

The goat said, "Better check the gas line," and scampered away.

The motorist was so frightened that he ran to the nearest farm house and told the farmer what had happened. "Was it an old goat with a floppy ear?" inquired the farmer.

"Yes! Yes!" cried the frightened man.

"Well, don't pay any attention to him," the farmer said. "He doesn't know anything about cars."

☛ A family was spending a weekend with relatives in the country. As they were being shown around the farm, the children came across a couple of goats and asked what they were.

Their father answered, "Why, those are goats."

Next in view was a battered old ewe, the veteran of several fights with the dogs. Suddenly, the three-year-old daughter spotted the ewe and screamed, "Look, Daddy, there's a goat with a sweater on!"

☛ A New York City businessman bought a sheep ranch in Montana. Come lambing time, a late blizzard hit the ranch.

The foreman wired the bad news to his boss in the Big Apple: "Blizzard is causing heavy lamb losses."

The owner acted with the vigor and promptness he had shown in the city business. He wired right back: "Stop lambing at once."

☛ A couple of goats wandered into an alley behind a movie house, searching for a bite to eat. They found a can of discarded movie film, and one of the goats devoured it.

"Well, how was it?" asked his companion.

"Not bad," he replied, munching on the last bite. "But the book was better."

Chapter 15

Going To The Dogs

"Perhaps it is only coincidence, but man's best friend can't talk."

☛ Three dogs were lost out in the woods. One dog belonged to a preacher, one to a gambler and one to a farmer.

The preacher's dog said, "I'll pray, and Heaven will show me the way home."

The gambler's dog said, "I'll just start out, and with some luck, I'll go the right way. I'll chance it."

The old farmer's dog said, "I'll just wait here. A government man should be here before long."

☛ "What kind of dog you got there, kid?" asked a passerby referring to the ugly mutt romping on the lawn with the young lad.

"He's a German police dog," the youngster proudly replied.

"He sure doesn't look like it to me," the stranger said, shaking his head.

"Course not," the little fellow said disdainfully."He's in the secret service."

☛ A city lady inspecting a litter of pups said, "I want a dog I can be proud of. Does this one have a good pedigree?"

"Listen, lady," the farm owner replied, "if he could talk, he wouldn't speak to either one of us."

☛ After weeks of painstaking effort, a hunter taught his retriever, Fido, to bring back ducks by walking on the surface of the water, rather than by swimming out after them. He wished to show off his "wonder dog" to a friend, so without speaking a word of his dog's newfound ability, they went hunting together.

When the hunter shot the first duck, he proudly sent Fido out to get it. The dog waltzed lightly on the water, retrieved the duck and walked back, dropping the bird at his master's feet.

"Notice anything?" the master asked his friend expectantly.

"Sure," answered the friend. "That crazy mutt of yours can't swim."

☞ A farmer took his Great Dane to the vet and said, "Doc, you've got to do something. My dog does nothing but chase sports cars on the highway."

"Well, that's only natural," the vet said. "Most dogs chase cars."

"Yes," the man agreed. "But mine catches them and buries them in the back yard."

☞ A nursery school sponsored a dog show and one four-year-old entered the family Basset Hound, Chester.

When the youngster returned from school, his mother asked how Chester fared in the contest.

"Well," he explained, "he almost won best of the breed, but then at the last minute, another Basset Hound showed up."

☞ "I feel so poorly lately—I'm tired all the time," said the farm dog.

"Have you thought of going to a psychiatrist?" asked his city cousin.

The first dog replied, "Heavens no! I'm not allowed on couches."

☞ The Texan was at it again. "And another thing," he said, "in Texas, we've got the fastest-running dogs in the world."

"Don't doubt it," the listener replied after pondering the thought, "the trees are so far apart."

☞ A stranger walking down the street heard a dog howling mournfully and decided to investigate. He found the dog sitting calmly on his haunches, but still emitting agonized yelps.

"What ails your dog?" he asked the hound's owner.

"Oh, he's lazy, that's all," answered the owner with no concern.

"But laziness doesn't make a dog howl!"

"No," agreed the owner, "but that darn dog is sitting on a sand-burr."

☛ Ad seen in a rural newspaper: "Lost farm dog. One ear gone from mower accident.

"Lost a leg chasing tractor. Part of tail missing from fight with pit bull. Cat got his left eye.

"Answers to the name, Lucky."

☛ A motorist was driving along a country road when he saw a huge sign, "Beware of Dog." Farther down was another "Beware of Dog" sign.

As he drove along, there was still another sign, "Beware of Dog."

Finally, he arrived at the farm house, and there was a tiny poodle standing in front of the house.

"Do you mean to say that little dog keeps strangers away?" he asked the farmer.

"No," replied the farmer, "but the signs do."

☛ The sales manager of a dog food company asked his sales force how they liked the company's advertising program.

"Great! Best in the business!" said one salesperson.

"And our new label and package?" asked the manager.

"Great! Best in the business!" said another.

"And what about our sales force?" the manager asked.

Since they were the sales force, they had to admit they were top-notch.

"OK, then," said the manager. "So if we've got the best label, best package, and the best advertising program being sold by the best sales force in the business, tell me, why are we in 17th place in the dog food business?" There was silence.

Finally, a rookie salesperson got up and said meekly, "Because the #X$*@?!X% dogs won't eat the stuff."

☛ It was Leon's sixth birthday. For months, he told his parents he wanted a dog more than anything else in the world. When he got home from school, his parents led him to the living room.

"Happy Birthday!" they said. "Say hello to your birthday present."

A full-grown St. Bernard sat in the middle of the room, looking at his new owners. Leon walked around the huge dog, being careful not to get too close. He stared at the enormous dog, while his parents waited for him to say something.

"Is anything wrong, Leon?" asked his father.

"No," Leon said. "Just tell me one thing. Is he for me, or am I for him?"

☛ Two puppies were watching a group of teenagers dancing. One turned to the other and said: "If we acted like that, they would worm us."

☛ A feed mill manager, who had four small children, brought a frisky puppy home one day to surprise the kids. They went wild and asked what they could name it.

His wife, who already had her hands full with four kids, offered a suggestion. "You'd better call it Mother," she said, "because if that dog stays, I'm going."

☛ A farmer walked into a local tavern with his dog, Alfred. Upon reaching his seat at the bar, he boasted that his dog could talk, and bet the bartender $20 that Alfred would speak. The bartender, eager to win the 20-spot, took him up on the bet.

"All right, dog, tell me what's on top of a house," the fellow said.

"Ruff," the dog replied.

The dog's answer irritated the bartender, who knew he'd been had. But then the farmer said he'd bet double-or-nothing that the dog could speak again, and the bartender agreed.

"Hey dog, who was one of the greatest baseball players ever to play for the New York Yankees?" the farmer asked.

"Ruff," said the dog, apparently intending to sound like New York Yankee great Babe Ruth.

This time, the bartender had enough and knocked the farmer from his barstool and picked both him and his mutt up and threw them out into the alley.

Alfred, the dog, feeling a bit perplexed, looked up at his owner and said, "Darn, I guess I should've said Joe DiMaggio."

☛ Ralph Armstrong had just moved into the neighborhood. His phone rang at three o'clock in the morning.

"Hello," the woman on the phone began, "This is Mrs. Burke next door. Your dog's barking is keeping me awake. If you don't do something about it, I'll call the police."

At three o'clock the next morning, Mrs. Burke's phone rang. Ralph Armstrong had called her back. "I just want you to know," he said, "that I don't have a dog."

☞ Two boys were talking. The first lad pointed to his dog and said: "He's the smartest dog in the world. Watch this. 'Bang! You're dead.'"

The other boy snickered, "He didn't do anything. He's just sitting there."

The first boy replied: "See how smart he is...he knows he's not dead."

☞ A man was walking down the street carrying a small dog under his arm when he was approached by the Larry, the town drunk.

"That's a fine lookin' poodle you've got yourself there, mister," the drunk slurred. "Where'd you get him?"

"I got him for my wife," replied the man.

Whereupon the drunk surveyed the dog more carefully and replied, "Well, I'd say that wasn't a bad trade."

Chapter 16

Playin' Fowl

"A bird in the hand may soil your sleeve, but as long as you got the bird in there, you don't have to worry about where your next meal is coming from."

—Fred Allen

☞ A farm mother returned from the chicken house and asked little Chuckie, "Do you know what happened to the eggs in the chicken house?"

"Sure I know," said Chuckie. "I put them in the dog house."

"Well, why did you do such a thing?"

"We want puppies," he answered, "not chickens."

☞ The hens who lived next door were constantly escaping through a hole in the fence of the chicken run and tearing up the Jones' property. The Jones protested, but their lazy neighbors never bothered to mend the hole.

As Jones returned from work one evening, he saw his neighbor hastily patching the wire fence. "I wonder what happened to finally get that lazy farmer to patch that darn hole," he said to his wife.

She smiled and said, "Well, I just put a few eggs under one of our bushes and made sure he saw me go out and collect them."

☞ Two old-timers were sitting on the porch when one said to the other, "Gosh, Barney, don't you wish we were barefoot boys again?"

"Not me," replied Barney. "I grew up on a turkey farm."

☞ A bunch of tall-tale-telling farmers were standing by the counter at the local elevator bragging about their farming expertise. "Speaking of hens," remarked one blowhard farmer, "reminds me of an old hen my dad once had. She

73

would hatch anything from a tennis ball to a lemon. Why one day she sat on a piece of ice and hatched two quarts of hot water."

"That doesn't even come close to a hen my mother once had," said another farmer. "By mistake they had been feeding her sawdust instead of ground corn. Well sir, she laid 12 eggs and sat on them and when they hatched, 11 of the chickens had wooden legs and the 12th was a woodpecker!"

☛ A mother, knowing that her children possessed an uncontrollable knack for uncovering secrets, decided desperate measures were needed to keep them from discovering this year's Easter eggs. So after coloring them, she took them out to the chicken house and put them under an old setting hen.

To her surprise, that afternoon she saw the rooster had returned and flew into a rage, jumped the fence and beat the living daylights out of the peacock.

☛ Two philosophical hens were sitting next to each other talking about life as chickens when one hen said, "Did it ever occur to you that with all the eggs we lay there ought to be more of us?"

☛ A frustrated farmer, who for some reason couldn't get fertile eggs, stumbled across an ad in the newspaper that read, "Super Rooster—$100."

Although the price was high, the farmer sent away for the rooster and set him loose in the hen house and watched as he zoomed in on every hen.

After he was finished, the farmer opened the hen house door and the super rooster raced out and took after the ducks and geese on the nearby driveway. Unable to catch the rooster, the farmer returned to the house for lunch.

As he was eating, he looked out the kitchen window and saw buzzards circling above the super rooster, who was lying on his back in the driveway. Fearing his expensive rooster was dead, he darted out to the driveway. When he knelt down to examine the rooster, the bird sat up, pointed to the circling buzzards and said, "Shhhh."

☛ When little Richie was sent across the street to fetch a cup of sugar, Mrs. Jones asked, "Tell me, Richie, what were all those chickens doing in front of your house this morning?"

He replied, "They heard someone say he was going to lay a sidewalk and they wanted to see how it was done."

☛ Two buxom hens were pecking away in the barnyard. Suddenly one of them looked over her shoulder and said to the other, "We'd better separate. Here comes that cross-eyed rooster again and we don't want him to miss both of us."

☛ Hubert, a poor poultry farmer who hadn't had much luck for years, suddenly turned great profits from egg production. A neighboring farmer asked, "After all those lousy years, what did you do?"
Hubert replied, "I put a sign up in the hen house."
"A sign? What did it say?"
"It read: 'An egg a day keeps Colonel Sanders away,'" Hubert said.

☛ A city girl was enjoying her first visit to the farm. She was quite impressed by the cows, pigs and chickens. When she saw the peacock, she was amazed, "Look," she gasped, "a rooster in full bloom."

☛ A lonely little chick making a turn around the electric incubator of unhatched eggs, frowned and said, "Well it looks like I'll be an only child. Mother's blown a fuse."

☛ A poultry farmer was having difficulty with his hens not laying and thought they needed encouragement. He had a parrot who could be taught to say anything, so he taught him to say, "Let's go girls, let's go," and put him in the hen house that night.
Next morning he went out eagerly to note the results. The parrot was high up on the ceiling, with nearly all his feathers plucked off and below stood a very angry rooster.
"Wait a minute, wait a minute," screeched the parrot. "I'm only here as a consultant."

☛ One farmer who owned two roosters complained one was so lazy he would nod when the other crowed each morning.

☛ "Tell me, class, why do ducks dive in the water?" the teacher asked during science class.
No one answered, until Jack threw his arm up into the air. "I know," he said proudly, "to liquidate their bills."

☞ A rooster was chasing a hen around the yard while the farmer sat on the front porch watching them. The farmer's wife stepped out the door, threw some corn out in the yard and went back into the house.

When the hen reached the corn, she hopped over it and kept running. The rooster reached the corn, suddenly screeched to a halt and began eating.

The farmer shook his head and said, "Lord, I hope I never get that hungry."

OK, you must have known these were coming:

☞ Why did the chicken only cross half of the road?
She wanted to lay it right on the line.

☞ Why did the chicken cross the playground?
To get to the other slide.

☞ There's a new game chickens are playing nowadays. They line up alongside a road and wait for a speeding car. Then, they all dash across in front of it and the last one to the other side is called a high school student.

☞ Two chickens were standing by the highway talking. The first chicken told his friend, "I'm telling you, Sam, if you cross that road, everyone will want to know why."

And now these:

☞ Did you hear about the farmer who crossed a dog with a chicken because he like pooched eggs?

☞ "What do you call a cross between a rooster and a duck?" the farm wife asked her husband.
"I don't know, what?" he said.
"I don't know either," she chuckled, "but whatever it is, it wakes you up at the quack of dawn."

☞ There once was an old far-sighted poultry scientist who tried to cross a rooster with a rooster. After relentless effort, all he got was two cross roosters.

Chapter 17

For The Birds...

"I suppose we shall go on regarding this thing as a much loved garden bird, even when it beats on the window with its beak and tells you to get that damn food out on the bird table, or else."

—Miles Kington

☛ A lonely elderly lady walked past the pet shop and saw a myna bird. She bought it to keep her company. The problem was, however, when she got it home, all it could say was, "My name is Roxie and I am a real swinger."

Well, the lady really liked the bird, but couldn't stand the language. She mentioned the problem to her parish priest and he said he had two extremely religious myna birds at the rectory.

"I even named them Peter and Paul," the priest said, "because they recite the rosary several times a day."

He suggested she bring her myna bird to the rectory. The priest believed that after a day or two of being influenced by his birds, Roxie would have a better demeanor.

So the lady took her bird to the rectory and, sure enough, the first thing it said was, "My name is Roxie and I am a real swinger."

There was silence from the priest's two myna birds until Peter turned to Paul and shouted, "Paul, toss out the beads. Our prayers have been answered."

☛ A telephone repairman knocked at the door of a farmhouse. "Come in," said a voice.

Inside, the repairman found only a parrot and a dog. As he debated whether to lecture the bird on the hazards of inviting in unknown guests, the parrot squawked to the dog, "Sic 'im!"

☛ The metal strips used to band birds are now inscribed, "Notify Fish & Wild Life Service, Washington D.C." because of the blunder of a midwest farmer. They used to read "Washington Biological Survey," which was abbreviated on the bands as: "Wash. Biol. Surv."

However, the old bands had to be changed after a disgruntled farmer who had shot a crow wrote to the U.S. Government: "Dear Sirs, I shot one of your pet crows the other day and followed instructions attached to it. I washed it and boiled it and served it. It was terrible! You should stop trying to fool people with things like that."

☛ A Texas oil tycoon was at a loss as to what to send his mother for her birthday. His brother got her an expensive sports car. He wanted to top that, so he paid $50,000 for a myna bird that could speak 11 languages and sing grand opera. He allowed time for the bird to arrive at its destination and then called his mother.

"What did you think of the bird, Mama?" he asked.

She replied, "Delicious!"

☛ A man purchased a parrot, and for five years tried in vain to get the bird to talk. He read books on the subject and bought records for the bird to listen to. Nothing happened. Disgusted, he decided to take him back to the pet shop.

As they crossed the street, a car was zooming right at them. The parrot yelled, "Look out!"

The car hit the man, knocking him to the ground. Only slightly bruised, he got up muttering something about "that dumb bird causing all my problems."

The parrot glared at him and said, "Who's dumb? For five years you try to get me talk, and then when I do, you won't listen."

☛ A recently widowed farmer was very lonely and went to the pet store to buy a talking bird as a companion.

The store owner sold him a talking bird for $435. The next day, the farmer returned and said the bird wouldn't talk. The owner sold him a bell and told the farmer to ring the bell to tune up the bird. The farmer paid the $55 for the bell and left.

The next day, the farmer returned again. The bird still hadn't said a word. So, the owner sold him a ladder for the bird—for $35. The farmer went home, but was back the next day because the bird still refused to talk. The store owner said he must need a swimming pool, and sold him one for $75.

On the fifth day, the farmer came in and yelled at the pet store owner, "I've now spent $600 and the bird's only words came just before he died."

The owner asks, "Well, what did he say?"

The farmer replied, "The bird said, 'Didn't that guy ever suggest you buy any birdseed?'"

☞ At an estate auction, a farmer bought a parrot for his wife after some very spirited bidding.

"Can the bird talk?" he asked the auctioneer.

The auctioneer laughed and said, "Who do you suppose has been bidding against you all this time?"

☞ A farm wife bought a parrot from the town pet shop, and was told that, with patience, it could be taught to talk.

So each day, she said, "Good morning," to the new bird in the house. But it never responded, even after several months.

One morning, not quite awake yet, the farm wife walked right by the bird without her usual greeting. The parrot eyed her coldly and squawked, "Well, what's the matter with you this morning?"

☞ A magician working a summer cruise ship had a pet parrot who often spoiled his act. The parrot was constantly saying to his audiences, "He has the card in his pocket," or "The card's up his sleeve," or "It went through a hole in his top hat."

The ship sank one day and the parrot and the magician found themselves together on a raft. For four days the parrot stared silently at the magician. Finally, on the fifth day, the parrot said, "OK, I give up. What did you do with the cruise ship?"

☞ What can a pigeon do that seven out of ten farmers cannot do?

Make a small deposit on a pickup truck.

☞ Because Leroy always complained he was too busy with work to spend time with his wife, she grew very attached to her pet parrot. But one day the parrot died, so she went into town to buy a new one. The pet store owner told her the only one left was from a tough gambling joint that was closed down. He said, "The bird is likely to say anything, coming from a place where there's booze, girls and bums."

The wife said, "That's OK, I'll retrain him."

Arriving home, she was surprised to see her husband. She carried the caged bird into the house and yelled, "Surprise!" to her husband and daughters.

When the cover came off the cage, the parrot looked around and said, "Well, whaddya you know—new joint, new madam, new girls. Same old customers. Hello, Leroy."

Life's A Zoo

"Some people lose all respect for the lion unless he devours them instantly. There is no pleasing some people."

—Will Cuppy

☞ The smash hit of the circus in the rural town was the beautiful lady lion tamer. She had the lions completely controlled. At her command, the fiercest lion of the bunch came up to her meekly, put his paws around her and nuzzled her shapely chest.

The crowd thundered its approval. Except one farmer stood and declared, "What's so great about that? Anybody can do it."

The ringmaster challenged him, "Would you like to try it?"

"You bet I would," replied the fellow. "But first get that lion out of here."

☞ A man was on his way to visit friends, and the path he traveled led through a swamp. "Say," he asked one of the other men in the group, "is it true that an alligator won't hurt you if you carry a torch?"

The man answered, "Well, I guess that all depends on how fast you carry it."

☞ There was a local tavern that owned a monkey that would often sit on a pickle barrel and play the harmonica. A patron saw that the monkey's tail was hanging in the barrel and told the bartender.

The bartender replied, "Don't bother me with it. Go tell the monkey."

Whereupon the patron approached the monkey and said, "Do you know your tail is hanging in the pickle barrel?"

"I don't know," replied the monkey, "hum a couple of bars and I'll see if I can pick up the melody."

☛ Two mice were launched in a missile from Cape Canaveral. The first mouse cried, "I'm scared. It's dangerous, you know, this space travel."

The second mouse turned to his friend and said, "Yeah, but it sure beats cancer research."

☛ Two farmers were walking across the frozen tundra when they were suddenly charged by an enormous polar bear. One of them started to put on his snowshoes and the other said, "What are you doing? You'll never outrun that bear."

The first farmer replied, "I don't have to. I just have to outrun you."

☛ A farm wife opened her refrigerator and there sat a rabbit, staring at her. The lady exclaimed, "What are you doing in here?"

The rabbit answered, "This is a Westinghouse, isn't it? I'm just 'westing.'"

☛ The lion sprang upon a bull and devoured him. After he had feasted, he felt so good that he roared. The noise attracted hunters and they killed him.

The moral of the story? When you are full of bull, you should keep your mouth shut.

☛ As the farmer read his monthly magazine, he called to his wife, "Just think, it says here that over 10,000 camels are used each year to make paint brushes."

"Goodness," answered the woman, impressed. "Isn't it amazing what they can teach animals these days?"

☛ The mother tiger opened her eyes lazily and saw her young son chasing a hunter around a tree.

"Junior," she called sharply, "how many times have I told you not to play with your food!"

☛ A mother mouse was taking her babies for a walk when suddenly, a cat appeared. The young ones were petrified, but the mother mouse huddled them behind her and started to bark with a loud, "Arf! Arf!" The cat took off immediately.

Then the mother mouse turned to her offspring and said, "Now children, that will teach you the value of learning a second language."

☛ A zoo manager was in real trouble because 200 school children were coming to see the gorilla, which was at the animal hospital with a toothache. Being as desperate as he was, the manager called a cage cleaner.

"I'll give you $100 if you'll dress up like a gorilla and swing around," he said.

"Sure!" the cleaner said. "I'll be right over."

The 200 kids arrived, all very excited about seeing the gorilla. So the man in the gorilla suit began to swing on the bars in the cage. He was swinging so hard that he lost his grip and fell into the lion cage, where he began to scream hysterically.

The lion put his paw over the man's mouth saying, "Shut up! You wanna get us all fired?"

☛ A bee was flying in the woods when suddenly a moose spotted the bee and ate him. The bee was inside, pretty mad and wanted to sting the moose. But after some thought, the bee decided it would take a lot of strength, so he took a nap first. When he woke up, the moose was gone.

MORAL: If you hesitate to make your feelings known, you may be left behind in the shuffle.

☛ The lady was visiting the mink farm and wishing to display her profound interest in the fur business, she asked brightly, "And how many skins do you get from each animal?"

"Only one, ma'am," the farmer replied. "It makes them nervous if we try to skin them twice."

☛ A lion was walking through the jungle declaring he was the king of beasts. He came to a zebra and roared, "Who is the king of beasts?"

The poor scared zebra said, "You are."

The lion continued walking until he came to a giraffe. He asked again, "Who is the king of beasts?"

The giraffe answered, "You are."

Next, the lion came to a buffalo and roared, "Who is the king of beasts?" Once again, the buffalo, shaking in its tracks, answered, "You are."

Then the lion came to an elephant and roared, "Who is the king of beasts?" The elephant grabbed the lion with his trunk, shook him three times and threw him against a tree.

The dazed lion got up and said, "Just because you didn't know the answer, you didn't have to get mad."

☞ A concerned young boy took his pet rabbit to the vet and said, "Doc, my rabbit's sick but all I fed him was goat's milk."

"Goat's milk!" the vet said with a smirk, "That's the problem. Don't you know that you never use greasy kid's stuff on your hare?"

☞ An enraged cowboy gazed down in contempt at the herd of buffalo he was guarding. "Buffalo!" he moaned. "The dirtiest, mangiest, nastiest bunch of critters I ever did see!"

One buffalo turned to another and said sadly, "Well, there it is, the one thing I thought I'd never hear—a discouraging word!"

☞ "I understand your father was a lion tamer, too," the TV newsman said to the lion tamer at the circus.

"Yes, he was," the lion tamer said.

"And did you ever put your head in the lion's mouth—the way your father did?" the interviewer went on.

The young lion tamer answered, "Only once—to look for Dad!"

☞ After the great flood, Noah told all the animals to leave the ark, go out into the world and multiply. However, he was surprised to see two small gray snakes stayed on board.

When he asked them why they didn't leave the ark, they replied, "We can't—we're Adders."

☞ An inventive furrier crossed a mink with a gorilla. The result? A beautiful coat, but the sleeves were too long.

☞ A Christian was thrown out into the Roman arena with a lion. He thought that if he could just communicate with the beast, his life would be spared. He started talking and a few moments later, he heard the lion mumbling.

"Thank God!" the Christian exclaimed, "we're communicating."

To which the lion replied, "I don't know about you, but I'm saying grace."

Weather-Beaten

"Sunshine is delicious, rain is refreshing, wind braces up, snow is exhilarating; there is no such thing as bad weather, only different kinds of good weather."

—*John Ruskin*

Chapter 19

Mother Nature Foolin' Around

"One weatherman had so much trouble with his forecasts that when he tried to get a jukebox to play 'Blue Skies,' it came up 'Stormy Weather.'"

☛ An agricultural college boy said to his roommate, "The drought back home must really be bad this time."
"How can you tell?" his roommate asked.
"I just got a letter from Dad," he said, "and the stamp was fastened on with a paper clip."

☛ Grandpa was telling about the terrible winter they had when he was a boy. "It was so cold," he said, "that the wolves were eating sheep just for the wool."

☛ A northern farm hand went to work for a Texas rancher. There had been a long dry spell and every man on the ranch was hoping for rain. One day it started to sprinkle and the farm hand, to show his delight, began to dance in the rain.
"Hey, you," shouted the ranch owner, "come in out of the rain!"
"Oh, I don't mind it a bit," the farm hand called back.
"That isn't the point," insisted the rancher. "I want every drop of that water to fall on Texas."

☛ Farmer Elliot was trying to convince everyone that he could forecast the weather by looking at his cows. If they were lying down, it was going to be clear. If they were on their feet and restless, it was likely to rain.
One of his hired hands challenged his theory and pointed out that some of his cows were lying down and others were

standing up. "Well," Elliot explained, "that just means it may rain and it may not."

☛ One local TV weatherman was wrong on his forecasts so often, he was publicly embarrassed and applied for a transfer. "Why do you wish to transfer?" the station manager asked. He replied, "The climate here doesn't agree with me."

☛ A traveling salesman, caught in a torrential storm, stopped overnight at a farmhouse. In the morning, he looked out and saw a flood tearing through the front yard.

He watched pieces of fence, chicken coops, branches and an old straw hat floating past in the rushing current. Then he saw the straw hat come back, this time moving upstream past the house! Then he saw it go down again. Pretty soon it came back upstream—and by now the salesman wondered if he had gone crazy. Finally, he called the farmer's daughter over.

"Oh," said the young girl as she looked out the window, "that must be Granddad. He said yesterday that in spite of hell or high water, he was going to mow the lawn today."

☛ A curious man called up his local weatherman and asked, "What are the chances for a shower tonight?"

The weatherman, a bit startled, answered, "Well, I'd say go ahead and take one if you really need it."

☛ The farmer took his wife to the doctor and said, "Doc, the cold weather has been affecting my wife's eyesight."

"Sorry to hear that, old man," said the doctor.

"So am I," the farmer said. "She's had visions of a fur coat."

☛ A summer tourist approached a farmer and asked, "Did you have much rain last year?"

"Not much," the farmer replied, "but my neighbor had more than I did."

"How could he?" inquired the astounded visitor.

The farmer answered, "He has more land than I have."

☛ A stranger, traveling through Kansas, got into a conversation with a farmer and his son at a filling station. "Looks like we might have rain," said the traveler.

"Well, I hope so," replied the farmer, "not so much for myself as for my boy, Buck, here. I've already seen rain."

☞ A Texan was visiting up north and struck up a conversation with a Minnesota farmer. "It gets so cold here in the winter that we have to put heaters under the cows to milk them," the Minnesotan said.

"That's nothing," said the unimpressed Texan. "It gets so hot back home in the summer that we have to feed the hens ice so they won't lay hard-boiled eggs."

☞ In the employee parking lot, two weather bureau forecasters were about to drive home.

"Say, Eugene," said one to the other, "Did you remember to close the office windows? Never know when it might rain."

☞ At breakfast, the farm wife said to her husband, "I think I will do a lot of shopping today. What is the weather going to be?"

Her husband looked up from his plate and said, "Rain, sleet, ice, snow, thunder, lightning and high winds."

☞ A violent earthquake hit the Indian reservation and the wise old chief was asked why. He told them, "You dance Sun Dance. Get sunshine. Dance Rain Dance. Get rain. Dance corn Dance. Get corn."

He waved his forefinger at them. "Now what you expect when everybody dance Twist?"

☞ Two farmers, one from Kansas and the other from Texas, were discussing poor crops, each outdoing the other in his pessimistic statement.

"Well," the Texan went on, "it's been a mighty poor year with hardly a drop of rain, but still not as bad as one I remember. That year, we ate 14 acres of corn at one sitting."

☞ A schoolmarm asked a weatherman's son, "How much are two and two?"

The weatherman's son answered, "There's a strong probability of four."

☞ Sitting around the diner, one blowhard farmer said, "One time it got so cold in the winter that they couldn't run the trains in my town."

"What are you talking about?" someone asked.

"Well," the old codger said, "the rails were huddling together to keep warm."

☞ A grandfather and his grandson were sitting on the milking parlor steps one hot summer afternoon talking about old times. The grandson looked at his grandfather and said, "You know, Grandpa, I believe this is the hottest summer that I've ever seen."

The grandfather said, "Yes, indeed, it is hot, but not like one summer when I was a boy."

"What do you mean?" the youngster inquired.

Grandpa replied, "It was so hot that the cows gave powdered milk."

☞ Prior to the 6 a.m. radio broadcast, the weather forecaster told the announcer, "Better break it to them gently. Just say, 'Partly cloudy, somewhat cooler, with heavy local showers, followed by a hurricane.'"

☞ One day a farmer went into the big city and decided to eat lunch at a sidewalk cafe. It rained so hard it took him one hour to finish his soup.

☞ A visitor to Oklahoma was talking to a sun-browned native and commented on the lack of rain. "Doesn't it ever rain here?" the visitor asked, wiping his forehead with the back of his hand.

The native thought a moment and said, "Mister, do you remember the story of Noah and the ark and how it rained for 40 days and 40 nights?"

"Sure I do," he answered.

"Well," drawled the Okie, "we only got a half-inch that time."

☞ "Just tell me, Doc," the weatherman said. "What are my chances for recovery?"

The doctor answered, "You have a 40% chance, increasing to 60% by Saturday."

☞ A North Dakota farmer looked at some ranch land in south Texas. The day he got there, they had an unbelievable 15 inches of snow.

The realtor was really upset, so he hired a teenage boy to tell the farmer that it was the first time in his life he'd ever seen snow.

Unfortunately for the realtor, the boy didn't stop there. He added, "But I've seen it rain twice."

☛ Two farmers, one from Michigan and one from Wisconsin, were recalling last winter's record cold spells and trying to outdo each other.

"It was so cold in Michigan," the first farmer said, "that the streakers in Detroit just described themselves to people."

Unimpressed, the Wisconsin farmer noted, "Well, it was a normal winter for us, but I did notice while hunting that the beagles were carrying jumper cables to get the rabbits started."

☛ The weather bureau received a postcard from a young farm boy that read, "Sirs: I thought you would be interested in knowing that I have just shoveled three feet of partly cloudy from my mom's front steps and driveway."

☛ An early-rising rancher's wife got out of bed one morning to check the weather and temperature. She reported, "It's cold, dismal and forty."

To which the cowman growled, "Who isn't?"

☛ Two weathermen were swapping jokes. One asked, "What is the Eskimo National Anthem?"

"I don't know, what?" his co-hort answered.

The first weatherman blurted, "'Freeze a Jolly Good Fellow.'"

☛ A weatherman was heard describing his wife to a friend. "She speaks 155 words a minute, with gusts up to 180."

☛ A 12-year-old schoolboy was expelled because his teachers claimed he wasn't capable of telling the truth. If this young man doesn't mend his ways, he is likely to end up in the weather bureau.

☛ Back in those terrible Depression days, a government farm agent touring the Great Plains wired back to Washington about an unusual creature he couldn't identify on the dry and drifting plains of South Dakota.

He described the creature: It had long whiskers, shuffling gait, was skinny, dehydrated and difficult to herd and handle. "What is it?" the agent queried.

A wire came back with this message: "That's the farmer, you darn fool!"

Courtship

"I was in love with a beautiful blonde once—she drove me to drink—'tis the one thing I'm indebted to her for."

—*W.C. Fields*

Chapter 20

Rural Romance

"Love is a grave mental disease."
—*Plato*

☛ A young farm boy was taking a girl to a dance for his first date. Seeing that he was extremely nervous, his mother began instructing him in the proper social graces.

"Remember," she said, "she will be just as nervous as you are. Say something nice to set her at ease."

As they started their first dance, the young lad remembered what his mother told him and finally said, "Boy, for a fat girl, you sure don't sweat much."

☛ "Oh honey," said young Tim to his girl, "since I met you I can't eat, I can't sleep and I can't drink."

"Why not?" she asked, thinking she would hear some flowery reason.

Instead Tim replied, "Because I'm broke."

☛ Charlie, a 20-year-old, complained to a friend that no matter what girl he brought home as a prospective bride, his mother expressed disapproval. The friend advised him, "Find a girl like your mother, then she's bound to like her."

Six months later, Charlie reported to his friend, "I took your advice. I found a girl who looked like my mother, talked like her and even cooked liked her."

"And what happened?" his friend asked.

"My father couldn't stand her," Charlie answered.

☛ Bob, who was a bachelor, was sulking at the bar. "I've never had any luck with women," he told the bartender. "I can remember when I was six years old, I told the little girl next door that I wanted to play doctor. She told me she was a Christian Scientist."

☞ Young Joan was looking very glum. "What's the matter, Joan?" asked her friend.

"It's my boyfriend," Joan explained. "He's lost all his money."

"Oh, no," her friend said. "I'll bet you're feeling sorry for him."

"Yes," said the young lady wistfully. "He's going to miss me."

☞ When Martha got to be 28 without any prospects of getting married to any farm boy in the vicinity, her nagging mother inserted an ad in the newspaper. The ad read: "Beautiful, exotic young heiress seeks companionship with devil-may-care gentleman who wants to go places fast."

After the ad appeared, the mother asked anxiously, "Well? Any answers?"

"Just one," the daughter replied.

"Who wrote it?" the mother asked.

"I shouldn't tell you," Martha said.

"But this was my idea," the mother shouted, "and I insist upon knowing."

"All right," Martha said, "You asked for it! It was Papa."

☞ A short-haired girl said to a long-haired boy on their first car date, "Of course Daddy doesn't mind our being alone together. He thinks you're a girl."

☞ A hillbilly just down from the mountains walked into a hotel with a dizzy blonde hanging on his arm. When asked by the hotel clerk to sign the register, he signed "X." But after a thinking a moment, he then circled the "X."

"A lot of people sign with an 'X,'" said the clerk, "but this is the first time I've ever seen one circled."

"Ain't nothing so darn strange about it," the hayseed drawled. "When I'm runnin' around with wild women, I don't use my right name."

☞ Courtship is the short space of time between lipstick and mopstick.

☞ The farm boy and the city girl were watching an old Jersey cow affectionately licking the face of a young heifer.

"Gee!" said the farm boy, "I'd like to be doing that."

"Go ahead," smiled the city girl. "It's your cow."

☛ "The time will come," thundered the lady orator at the Women's Lib meeting, "when women will get men's wages."

"Yeah," a man who was sitting with his girl in the back row muttered, "it'll happen this weekend."

☛ A young man had been courting a young girl for some time and constantly tried at no avail to get her consent to marriage. He finally confided to her that "my elderly father is quite ill and will probably die soon. When that happens I will be a millionaire."

Two days later, the girl became his stepmother.

☛ "Mr. Arnold," the timid-looking farm boy began, "er—um, that is, can, er, will you..."

"Why, yes, my boy, you may marry her," said Mr. Arnold with a smile.

"What?" exclaimed the boy. "Marry who?"

"My daughter, of course! That is what you meant, isn't it?" he asked. "You want to marry her, don't you?"

"Er, that's not it," said the farm boy. "I just wanted to know if you'd lend me $20."

"Certainly not!" said Mr. Arnold. "Why, I hardly know you!"

☛ Two girls were discussing their boyfriends. One said, "My Tim's so cheap—the only restaurant we ever go to is the Stillwater Steak House."

"Cheap?" the other answered. "Hank told me that steak was an endangered species."

☛ A boy and a girl were out driving in the country one evening. They came to a quiet spot on a deserted lane and the car stopped.

"Oops," the boy said, "out of gas."

The girl opened her purse and pulled out a bottle.

"Wow!" the boy said as his eyes lit up. "A bottle—what is it?"

The girl answered, "Gasoline."

☛ "It's one o'clock in the morning," the angry father said to the young fellow keeping his daughter company on the porch. "Do you think you can stay here all night?"

"Gee, sir, I don't know," the boy replied. "I'll call home and ask."

☞ Buck, a swinging rancher, had a roving eye for a pretty girl. He was having a shave in the barber shop when a very pretty manicurist came up and began fixing his nails.

Buck asked, "What will you do, baby, when you get through with work?"

"I suppose I'll go home," the young beauty answered.

"Well," said Buck, "why not go out with me and we will kick up our heels and have a big ol' time?"

She replied nonchalantly, "Well, you'll have to ask my husband."

"Where is he?"

"He's shaving you!"

☞ A young farmer was boasting about his current girlfriend. "You should see my girl," he said. "She's as pretty as a mirage."

"That's the wrong simile," his friend told him. "A mirage is something you see but you can't get your hands on."

"That's my girl," the chap replied.

☞ The pretty young farm girl had just broken off her engagement with a young doctor.

"Do you mean to tell me," exclaimed her girlfriend, "that he actually asked you to return all his presents?"

"Not only that," she replied, "but he sent me a bill for 44 house calls."

☞ The girl's father had a serious talk with her boyfriend. "I've made my final decision," the father began. "I don't want my daughter dependent on a hopeless idiot for the rest of her life."

"Of course not, sir," the boyfriend said. "Then I take it we have your consent?"

☞ A stolen kiss frequently leads to marriage, which proves crime doesn't pay.

☞ At the school dance where dancing consisted of twisting, stomping and twirling around in circles, the music abruptly stopped. As a youth walked off the dance floor and over to the side, a girl rushed up to him and thanked him for the dance.

"I wasn't dancing," the boy hastily replied. "I was just trying to get past you to the Coke machine."

☛ The young lad looked and looked for a long time before he found a girl he could take home to meet his mother.

"Mom, this girl is great," he said. "She loves to cook, she loves to sew, she takes care of the house—she does everything!"

"Wonderful," said the mother enthusiastically. "I'll use her on Tuesdays and Thursdays."

☛ During the unfortunate breakup, the boy said, "But last night you said there was something you liked about me."

She answered, "Yes, there was, but you spent it all."

☛ A father took her daughter's boyfriend for a walk around the farm. "So tell me," he said, "are your intentions toward my daughter honorable or dishonorable?"

The boy's eyes lit up. "You mean I have a choice?"

☛ "I don't see why you're so mad at your ex-fiancee," said one of the hired hands. "After all, she returned your ring."

"That's right," replied the other. "But she didn't have to mail it back, marked, 'Glass, handle with care!'"

☛ A young farm lady brought a boy home to meet her parents. When the young girl left, the girl's father told his daughter he didn't approve of the lad.

"But," pleaded the girl, "Harry doesn't smoke, drink or gamble. He always attends church on Sunday. Now what can you find wrong with him?"

The father stood scratching his head, then replied, "You can never trust a liar."

☛ Courtship: The period during which the girl decides whether or not she can do any better.

☛ "I'm not wealthy," young Richard confessed, "and I don't have a new sports car and a yacht like Bill Turner, but I love you with all my heart."

"I love you, too," replied the girl. "But tell me more about Bill Turner."

☛ Young Earl looked at the high prices on the night club menu and cringed. Thinking quickly, he turned to his date and said, "What will you have, my lovely plump little doll?"

96

☞ "Sir, I'd like permission to marry your daughter," the young boy asked.

The father replied, "Hmmmm, do you really think you can support her on a hundred bucks a week?"

"I suppose so," said the suitor, "if that's all you can afford."

☞ Grandpa says it's still easy to tell the sexes apart despite the fact that nowadays men wear long hair and women wear pants. The one listening is the man.

☞ Marvin was a playful middle-aged buck who, standing close to an attractive blonde on the bus, inquired, "Where have you been all my life?"

She looked him over cooly and replied, "Well, for the first half of it, I wasn't even born!"

☞ Before his daughter's date, the father asked, "Lucy, does this boyfriend of yours have any money?"

"You men are all alike," Lucy replied. "That's what he asked about you!"

☞ Two hired hands were talking as they rounded up the cattle. "I was out with a new girl last night," Al said.

"Oh?" the other replied. "What's she like?"

"Everything," Al answered, shaking his head. "Filet mignon, potatoes, lobster, salad, ice cream—everything."

☞ A young man approached the counter where greeting cards were sold. "Have you anything sentimental?" he asked.

"Here's a lovely one," said the salesgirl. "It says, 'To the only girl I ever loved.'"

"That's beautiful," the young man said. "I'll take four."

☞ The young lady from a farming community told her friend she had decided to marry Winston, a rather eccentric millionaire.

"But," her friend said, "everybody thinks he's a little bit cracked."

"He may be cracked," the young lady said, "but he certainly isn't broke."

☛ A girl walked up to her fiance and said, "Here's your ring. I can't marry you. I love someone else."

"Who is he?" her boyfriend answered.

"You're not going to kill him, are you?" she asked nervously.

No," he said. "I just want to sell him the ring."

☛ The farm hand was on a rather romantic date with his girlfriend and said, "Honey, I am keeping a record of all the good times we've had together."

"Oh," she gushed, "you're keeping a diary."

"No," he said, "just the stubs in my checkbook."

'Till Death Do Us Part

"Marriage is a great institution, but I'm not ready for an institution."

—Mae West

Chapter 21

The Honeymoon's Over

*"One good thing about living
on a farm is that you can fight
with your wife without being heard."*
—Kin Hubbard

☞ A young boy asked his mom, "Mom, how long can someone live without a brain?"
Mother looked puzzled for a moment. "I don't know," she said. Then she turned toward her husband and said, "Honey, just how old are you anyway?"

☞ Two men at the local grain elevator were talking. "My wife thinks she should have a dish-washing machine," said one.
"You're lucky," the other answered. "My wife thinks she married one."

☞ A farmer came home from town one day and said to his wife, "Pack your bags! I just won the lottery!"
His wife asked, "But what should I pack, summer clothes or winter clothes?"
"Pack all of them," he said, "you're out of here!"

☞ At the family reunion, a distant aunt came up to Mary Sue. "It's been a long time since I've seen you," the woman said. "Are you married?"
"Yes," Mary Sue replied.
"But if I remember correctly," the aunt said, "you used to say you wouldn't marry the best man on earth."
To which Mary Sue answered, "I didn't."

☞ "Stick to the washing, ironing, scrubbing and cooking," the grumpy farm husband said to his wife. "No wife of mine is going to work."

☞ During one of their frequent squabbles, Floyd told his wife that she didn't deserve a husband like himself. She said, "I don't deserve arthritis, either, but I have it."

☞ At the town bar, one farmer complained, "My wife is always finding my money no matter where I hide it."

"My wife never finds mine," the other farmer answered. "I put it in the basket with my undarned socks."

☞ "Henry," his wife asked, "when did you first realize you loved me?"

Henry answered, "When I started getting mad at people who said you were fat, dumb and ugly."

☞ A retired farm couple was reminiscing on the front porch. As they exchanged memories, things began to get sentimental.

"You know, Sarah, you've always been with me. Like the time I was drafted—you became a nurse so you could be with me. When I was wounded—you were there by my side. Then I lost everything in the depression—and you were still with me. And when I lost the farm eight years ago, you were with me.

"And now, here I am, old and sick and still poor—and here you are right beside me," the old farmer said. "You know something, Sarah? You're bad luck!"

☞ A young farm husband was terribly disappointed when his wife gave birth to a baby daughter. "But why?" his friend asked.

He confided, "I was hoping for a boy to help me with the housework."

☞ A farmer's wife woke her husband Morton one morning and said, "Today's our 40th wedding anniversary. I think we ought to celebrate. What do you say we cook one of our chickens?"

"Why in the world," Morton asked, "do you want to punish a poor chicken for something that happened 40 years ago?"

☛ A farmer rushed into the farm house all out of breath and yelled at his wife, "Our marriage is illegal!"

His shocked wife asked, "What do you mean?"

He explained, "Your father didn't have a permit to carry that gun."

☛ "It's odd," the man told his wife Martha at a dinner party one night, "but the biggest idiots seem to marry the prettiest women."

"Oh, now," Martha said, "you're just trying to flatter me."

☛ When the engine on his airplane died, the pilot was forced to parachute out. On his way down, he passed a woman going up. He called, "Lady, have you seen an airplane on its way down?"

"Why no," she called back to him. "Have you seen a gas range on its way up?"

☛ The chief effect of love is to drive a man half-crazy; the chief effect of marriage is to finish the job completely.

☛ Nervous Ernie joined the Toastmasters, but really hated giving unrehearsed speeches, which is part of the training. He stepped up to the podium and in his envelope was the topic, "sex." He was to give a five-minute impromptu speech on the subject.

Ernie did a fabulous job, and even received a standing ovation at the end. At home that night, his wife asked what his speech was about. Too bashful to say "sex," he told her he spoke on "waterskiing."

Next week at the Toastmasters' picnic, someone came up to her and said, "You should have seen your husband perform last week—he did a super job."

Still unaware of the actual topic, she said, "I don't see how—he doesn't know hardly anything about it. As far as I know, Ernie's only tried it twice, and he fell off both times."

☛ "Darling," asked the proud young bride after serving her first meal at home, "what will I get if I cook you a dinner like this every day for a year?"

"My life insurance," he grumbled. "And it won't take a year."

☞ The farmer had been lecturing his five-year-old Sally for several minutes. Her conduct had been inexcusable.

She stood in silence, then eyed her daddy very seriously and said, "Daddy, don't think that just because you married Mommy, you have a right to be rude to all women."

☞ During the family health checkups with Dr. Phillips, the physician said to the farm wife, "To be honest, I don't like the looks of your husband."

She replied, "I don't either, but he's good to me and the kids."

☞ After several months of married life, the glamour wore off and the young farm couple went to see a counselor. After talking with the couple for a while, the counselor suddenly swept the woman into his arms and kissed her passionately.

"Now," said the marriage counselor. "This is the treatment your wife needs...Monday, Thursday and Saturday, at least."

"OK," replied the husband. "I can bring her in here on Thursday and Saturday nights, but Monday is my bowling night."

☞ Some say getting married is a lot like going into a restaurant with a friend. You order what you want, then when you see what the other fellow has, you wish you'd gotten that.

☞ A farm woman bought a new wig and thought it would be a good joke to surprise her husband at the bar in town. She strolled into the bar and asked him, "Do you think you could find a place in your life for a woman like me?"

"Not a chance," he snapped. "You remind me too much of my wife."

☞ A farmer appeared at a newspaper office to place an ad offering a $500 reward for the safe return of his wife's pet cat.

"That's an awful steep price to pay for a cat," the clerk said.

"Not this one," replied the farmer. "I drowned it."

☞ A husband turned to his wife and said, "How can you be so incredibly beautiful and so incredibly stupid at the same time?"

"It's God's will," the clever wife retorted. "He made me incredibly beautiful so that you could be attracted to me and made me incredibly stupid so I'd be attracted to you."

☞ A school teacher who was explaining to her class that women normally live longer than men, asked if anyone could tell her a reason.

"Yes," said the small boy. "They don't have wives."

☞ At the dinner table, Judy said to her husband, "I think I'll join the Women's Lib movement. They are advocating that a man pay his wife for doing housework."

"Sounds good to me," her husband said. "I'll pay you $25 a day—but I only need you to come in on Thursdays."

☞ "What's the matter, Thomas?" asked a friend at the office. "You look terrible!"

"If you only knew!" moaned Thomas. "The I.R.S. left a message that they called today. I just know I'm going to be audited again. Then the boss left a message that he wants to see me first thing Monday morning. There have been staff cuts in my department and I know I'm the next to go. Then my wife called and said she's leaving me for a chimpanzee. My whole life is in ruins!"

Thomas' friend worried about him all weekend and decided to stop by and see him the following Monday. He found Thomas smiling and chatting with his fellow employees.

"I'm really sorry about last Friday," Thomas said privately. "I was upset for nothing. I saw the boss and he gave me a raise. The I.R.S. found an error in my tax return and I'm going to get a fat refund this year!"

"That's great, Thomas, but what about your wife?"

"That's my fault, too," he said, "I never should've married a chimpanzee."

☞ "My sister married a man in the fire department," a youth told a friend.

"Volunteer?" the friend inquired.

The youth replied, "Nope. Pa made him."

☞ "No doubt about it," said one farm wife to another, "my husband's a perfect angel."

"You're lucky," her friend said, "mine's still alive."

☞ On their wedding night, the groom was terribly nervous. When he went into the bathroom to change and was taking off his socks, he remembered he had to tell his new bride his secret—his feet stunk terribly.

He worried and fretted, but he couldn't come up with a solution, so he just went back to the bedroom and hopped into bed.

His bride went into the bathroom next and as she was brushing her teeth, she remembered her horrifying secret—terrible breath. But she didn't know how to tell her husband, so she finally decided that she would just get into bed and tell him.

As she got into bed, she turned to him and said, "Darling, I have something I must tell you."

Horrified, he looked at her and screamed, "You ate my socks!"

☞ A farmer was talking to his hired hand while milking. "My wife got a terrific new mudpack treatment at the beauty parlor last week," the farmer said.

"Did it work well?"

"Yeah," the farmer said. "It worked great for three days, but then the mud fell off."

☞ A man was being interviewed for a job at the office and was asked how he'd feel about having a woman boss. He hesitated, but then said, "Well, I guess I'd feel at home."

☞ The wife was reading her husband's fortune on a weight card at the carnival. "It says you're dynamic, a leader of men and admired by women for your good looks and strength of character," she said. "It got your weight wrong, too."

☞ After returning from a week at her mother's, the farm wife was visited by a neighbor. "Do you think your husband minded keeping the house while you were away?" she asked.

"He says not," the wife said, "but I notice the parrot is doing a lot more swearing these days."

☞ "My husband didn't leave a bit of insurance," Louise told her neighbor.

"Then where did you get that gorgeous diamond ring?"

"Well," said Louise, "he left me $1,000 for a casket and $5,000 for a stone. This is the stone."

☞ If it's true that daughters are inclined to marry men like their fathers, it's understandable why so many mothers cry at weddings.

☛ At a huge wedding reception, a farmer gave a woman a big hug by mistake. When he saw his error he said, "No offense intended, madam, I thought you were my wife."

"A fine husband you must be," she snorted, "you over-stuffed, miserable, incompetent lout!"

"You see," exclaimed the farmer, "you even talk like her!"

☛ You can say this about marriage—it teaches you loyalty, forebearance, self-restraint, meekness and many other qualities you wouldn't need if you were single.

☛ Farmer Fred was overheard saying, "I just discovered a new birth control device. My wife takes off her makeup."

☛ The angry husband said to his wife, "My shaving brush is stiff—do you know why?"

"I sure don't, dear," his wife replied. "It was nice and soft when I varnished the bird cage with it yesterday."

☛ At the 4-H Parents' party, the young wife whispered to her husband, "That's the fourth time you've gone back for more cake and ice cream. Doesn't it embarrass you?"

"Why should it?" asked the husband. "I keep telling them it's for you."

☛ The men were at it again, telling stories about their wives. "Talk about ugly," Wayne said, "One time I took a Polaroid picture of her and it refused to develop!"

☛ A friend approached Tim and said, "I hear you advertised for a wife. Any replies?"

"Sure," Tim said. "Hundreds."

"What did they say?"

Tim answered, "They all said, 'Here, take mine.'"

☛ A farmer's wife was shopping at the grocery store. Browsing through the produce aisles, she said to the grocer, "Give me a pound of those grapes—my husband likes them. Do you know if they've been sprayed with any kind of poison?"

"No, ma'am," the grocer replied. "You'll have to get that at the hardware store."

☛ When the farmer began his chores as usual on the morning of his 25th wedding anniversary, his chatterbox wife was extremely annoyed. "Don't you realize what day this is?" she demanded.

"Sure I do!" he retorted.

"Well, in that case," persisted his wife, "let's do something unusual."

The farmer thought for a moment, and then suggested hopefully, "How about five minutes of complete silence?"

☛ Looking worried, a farmer hurried into a flower shop and asked to see the potted geraniums.

"I'm sorry," said the florist. "We haven't any potted geraniums, but we have a nice selection of African violets on sale today."

"No, no, not violets," he said. "It was a geranium my wife asked me to water while she visited our grandchildren."

☛ The farmer said to his wife, Janet, "Well, my dear, I've carried you safely over all the rough spots of life, haven't I?"

"Yes," Janet said, "and I don't think you missed one of them."

☛ Two farmers whose wives dragged them to the shopping mall were talking. The first said, "Did you know that most married men are a lot like politicians?"

The other farmer said, "How's that?"

"Well," Albert said, "they lay down the law and then have to accept all of their wives' amendments."

☛ Sleeping soundly in the upper berth of the train's sleeping car, a gentleman was awakened by a persistent tapping from below.

"Oh, Mr. Bailey, are you awake?" asked the middle-aged lady in the bunk below.

"I am now," he said groggily.

"It's frightfully cold down here, Mr. Bailey," she said. "I wonder if you would mind getting me a blanket."

"I've got a better idea, lady," he said. "Let's pretend we're married."

He could hear her giggling softly below him. "Oh," she said, "that sounds like a lovely idea."

"Good," he said, rolling over. "Now go get your own #@&*%$ blanket!"

☛ Two farm wives were talking at the hairdresser. "My husband was named Man-of-the-Year," one woman bragged.

"Well," said another lady, "that just shows you what kind of year it's been."

Chapter 22

Guess Who's Coming For A Visit?

*"I haven't spoken to my
mother-in-law for 18 months—
I don't like to interrupt her."*

—*Ken Dodd*

☛ The entire rural community was shocked when Zeke's mule kicked his mother-in-law to death. Just before the minister was about to start the funeral service, he said to Zeke, "She must have been a wonderful woman. Look at all the men who have left their work to attend the funeral."

"They ain't here to attend the funeral," Zeke said. "They all want to buy the mule."

☛ "If your mother hates Roger so much, why did she consent to your marrying him?" one of the bride-to-be's friends asked.

"Well," the young woman said, "she says she's looking forward to being his mother-in-law."

☛ A woman was overheard at the supermarket, "Our son and daughter-in-law came up with a foolproof way to save money on food. They bought themselves an economy car and began driving it to our house for dinner."

☛ "George, you're a liar," the boss yelled. "You took a day off to bury your mother-in-law and I met her last night in the supermarket."

George shamefully admitted, "Oh, I didn't say she was dead. I just said I would like to go to her funeral."

☛ Some men are willing to split the blame for a failed marriage—half his wife's fault, half her mother's.

☛ The young groom said to his new wife, "I'm beginning to suspect that your mother has a low opinion of me."

"Whatever makes you say that?"

"You know those towels she gave us," he said, "well, they're marked 'Hers' and 'Idiot's.'"

☛ A mother took her daughter's steady boyfriend out onto the porch for a serious talk. "So, Ryan," she said, "you want to become my son-in-law?"

He answered, "No, ma'am, not really. But if I marry your daughter, I don't see how I can avoid it."

☛ Two farm wives were discussing marriage. One said, "I bet Adam and Eve had a good married life."

Her friend asked, "Why do you think that?"

"Well," came the answer, "he couldn't wish she could cook like his mother and she couldn't fuss about all the other men she might've married."

☛ A farm husband and wife were quarreling about each other's relatives. "You haven't one good thing to say about any of my relatives," the husband shouted.

"Oh, yes I have," she replied. "I like your mother-in-law better than mine."

☛ On his birthday, James received two ties for his birthday from his mother-in-law. When he appeared at her house the next week wearing one of the new birthday ties she gave him, he was greeted with: "What's the matter, didn't you like the other one?"

☛ Harold was overheard telling the guys at the bar, "Whoa, boy, have I got troubles. My wife left me three weeks ago and my mother-in-law stayed."

☛ One farmer said to his neighbor, "I should've known I was in trouble the moment I got married. My wife's mother and father sent me a thank you note."

☛ One of life's greatest mysteries is how that idiot that married your daughter can be the father of the smartest grandchildren in the world.

☞ After griping about his mother-in-law for 15 minutes, Ted said, "But I will say this for her—there was one time in my life when I think I would have cut my throat if it wasn't for my mother-in-law."

"How do you mean?" Pete asked.

Ted answered, "She was using my razor to shave her mustache."

☞ There's a new product on the market today to make an angel of your mother-in-law. It's called cyanide.

☞ The farm mother was talking about her family. "Only one thing keeps my daughter from being happily married," she told her friend. "Her husband."

☞ "If I had to do it over again," remarked the weary husband, "I'd marry a Japanese girl. They're pretty, graceful, loyal—and your mother-in-law is in Yokohama."

☞ Two farmers were out playing golf one day when one said, "I'm eager to make this shot because that's my mother-in-law on the clubhouse porch."

His friend replied, "That's silly, it's over 200 yards and you surely can't expect to hit her from here."

☞ An old country woman was riding the bus on the way to visit her daughter and her husband. She was reading about birth and death statistics in the newspaper. Poking the man next to her, she said, "Do you know that every time I breathe, someone dies?"

"Very interesting," the man replied. "Have you tried using mouthwash?"

☞ A husband brought his dog to the veterinarian and asked that the dog's tail be cut off right at the rear.

"I can't do that," the vet said. "Why would you want to do such a thing to that innocent dog?"

"My mother-in-law is visiting next week," he explained. "And I want to eliminate any possible signs of welcome."

☞ One more reason the Mormon idea of polygamy didn't spread much was because it also multiplied in-laws.

☛ Two old mountain women were sitting on the porch and one was showing the other her shotgun. The other woman looked at the rusty old relic with an admiring grin.

"That gun," the hillbilly woman said, "has killed more game—possums, coons, groundhogs, squirrels, quail and stuff like that...

"But what's more," she observed under her breath, "it's got me two sons-in-law."

☛ "But I can't marry him, Mother," the soon-to-be bride cried. "He's an atheist and doesn't even believe in Hell."

"Marry him, my dear," her mother said, "and between the two of us, we'll convince him."

Chapter 23

For Better
Or For Worse...

*"Never go to bed mad. Stay up and
fight."*

—Phyllis Diller

☞ A farm woman was telling her side of the story to the
marriage counselor. "For 25 years," she began, "my husband
and I were very happy."
"Then what happened?" the counselor said gently.
She replied, "We met."

☞ "I remember my wedding day so distinctly," the elderly
farmer told his neighbor. "I brought my bride home to the
little house I bought, carried her over the threshold and said,
'Honey, this is your world and this is my world.'"
"And I suppose you lived happily ever after?" asked the
other man.
"Well, not exactly," replied the other grimly. "We've been
fighting for the world's championship ever since."

☞ There was a fellow who died and went right to Heaven
but found two lines at the Pearly Gates. Over one line a sign
read: "Men who were dominated by their wives." Over the
other line was a sign that read: "Men who were not dominated
by their wives."
The 'dominated' line was stretched back for miles. At the
other entrance stood a scrawny little fellow—alone.
The new arrival went over and asked the little fellow,
"What are you doing in this line?"
The little fellow replied, "My wife told me to stand here."

☞ "I was married twice," explained Boyd to a new acquaintance, "and I'll never marry again. My first wife died after

eating poisoned mushrooms and my second wife died of a fractured skull."

"That's a shame," said the friend. "How did that happen?"

Boyd replied, "She wouldn't eat her mushrooms."

☞ A farm couple was having a terrible fight. "You're homely as sin," the husband shouted.

"And you're drunk," she yelled back.

"Maybe so," he replied, ducking a few dishes thrown at him, "but I'll be over that in the morning!"

☞ When the henpecked farmer died and went below, he immediately started throwing his weight around and giving orders to everybody.

"Say, buddy," roared Satan, "you act as though you own this place."

"I do," replied the newcomer. "My wife gave it to me while I was on earth."

☞ Gordie, all depressed, was sitting at the bar staring at his drink. "What's the matter, Gordie?" the bartender asked.

"Same old thing," Gordie said.

"Why don't you drown your sorrows?" the bartender asked.

"I can't," Gordie said. "It's against the law—and besides, she's stronger than I am."

☞ Two farmers were talking to each other when one of them asked, "Can a man make a fool of himself without knowing it?"

"Not if he has a wife," replied the other.

☞ After a long day of work in the fields, Hank was surprised there wasn't any food on the table. When he questioned his wife, she quickly replied, "I went to a Women's Lib meeting and I don't have to fix supper all the time!"

To the farmer's own amazement, he said, "OK, I'll fix it myself."

Just before finishing his meal, his wife returned to the kitchen explaining that she didn't have to do dishes all the time. "OK," Hank said, "I'll do them."

After finishing the dishes, Hank settled back in the easy chair to watch the football game. With two seconds left on the clock with the score tied at 14-14, his favorite team was about to line up for a field goal when his wife charged in and changed the channel.

He said, "What do you think you're doing?"

"I don't have to watch football if I don't want to," she replied.

Then Hank said, "Enough is enough. What would you think if you didn't see me for a week?"

She said, "That would be all right with me."

So Tuesday she didn't see him and Wednesday she didn't see him. On Thursday she still couldn't see him, but on Friday she could just barely see him out of her right eye!

☞ Two fertilizer salesmen were talking at an out-of-town convention. "Does your wife miss you much?" asked the first.

"No," said the other. "She throws a pretty straight rolling pin for a woman."

☞ Today's divorce rate continues to spiral upward. It seems what more and more people want out of marriage...is to get out.

☞ A salesman and a psychologist were making small talk at a party. "You and your wife seem to get along very well," said the salesman. "Do you ever have differences of opinion?"

"Definitely," answered the psychologist, "but we always get over them quickly."

"How do you do that?"

"Simple," said the psychologist. "I never tell her about them."

☞ Rudy was feeling down in the dumps and a couple of farmers stopped to ask him what was the matter. "My wife told me she wouldn't talk to me for 30 days."

"But that's great," said the farmers, "Why are you complaining?"

"You don't understand," Rudy said. "Tomorrow's the last day."

☞ A farmer's wife complained to her husband, "Look at the clothes I have to wear—if anyone came to visit they would think I was the cook!"

"Well," her husband replied, "they'd change their minds if they stayed for dinner."

115

☞ A tired farmer's grueling day in his fields was capped off by his wife's announcement that the cleaning lady had walked out. "What was the trouble this time?" he asked wearily.

"You were!" she charged. "She said you used insulting language to her over the phone this morning."

"Good grief," cried the husband, "I thought I was talking to you!"

☞ A motorcycle policeman was writing up a ticket charging a farmer with speeding on the freeway to town, when a woman in the back seat went into a tirade.

"There!" she said. "Didn't I tell you to watch out? But you kept right on speeding, getting out of line, not blowing your horn, passing stop signs, and everything else. Didn't I tell you you'd get caught? Didn't I?"

"Who is this woman?" asked the officer.

"My wife," the farmer said grimly.

"Drive on, my friend!" exclaimed the cop as he proceeded to tear up the ticket. "Drive on, and may the Lord have mercy on you!"

☞ A tourist in the Ozarks saw a mountain farmer struggling hand-to-hand with a huge bear. He was about to find help when he saw the man's wife calmly standing on a stump, rifle in hand.

"Why don't you shoot the beast?" he asked.

"I will if I have to," she replied calmly, "but I'm waiting to see if the bear won't save me the trouble."

☞ Mabel tried to get her husband to quit drinking. One night, she dressed up like a hideous demon to scare the living daylights out of him.

When Joe came home after making his usual rounds, she jumped out and screamed. He took it all in stride and said, "You can't scare me—I married your sister."

☞ A farmer and his wife had a fight in the car and hadn't spoken for many miles. They'd quarreled and neither would budge. Suddenly, the man pointed to a mule in the pasture.

"Relative of yours?" he asked.

"Yes," his wife replied. "By marriage."

☞ Little Alexander was reading from his Sunday school book at the breakfast table. He read, "God created man and then woman."

Confused, he asked his father why and he responded, "He did it that way because he didn't want any advice while creating man."

Hearing her husband's response from the kitchen, the mother said, "Your father's wrong, Alex. God did it that way because he wanted a rough draft before making all the improvements."

☞ "What do you mean coming home half-drunk?" the angry farm wife asked.

"It wasn't my fault," replied her husband. "I ran out of money."

☞ The psychiatrist advised his timid patient to assert himself. "Don't let your wife bully you. Go home and show her who's boss," he said.

The patient went home, slammed the door loudly and roughly seized his wife.

"From now on," he snarled, "you're taking orders from me, see? You're gonna make my supper this minute, and when it's on the table, you're going upstairs to lay out my clothes. See? Tonight I'm going out on the town—alone. And do you know who is going to dress me in my tuxedo and black tie?"

"You bet I do," was her answer, "the undertaker!"

☞ A farmer asked his wife what she would like for her birthday. "A divorce!" she replied.

"Ouch," he said, "I hadn't planned on spending that much."

☞ "Marvin is so forgetful," the farm wife complained to a visitor. "He forgets his coat, keys—even his address. I sent him out for some lemons just now, and I don't know if he'll remember to come home."

As the visitor sympathized with the wife, Marvin burst into the living room.

"You'll never guess what happened to me! An old eccentric was passing out money on the street, and look what he handed me!"

He opened a fistful of $100 bills.

"See?" said the wife. "He forgot the lemons."

☞ "Daddy, what's the difference between a shotgun and a machine gun?" the little tyke asked.

"There is a big difference, Eddie," said his father. "It is just as if I spoke, and then your mother spoke."

☞ A drunk staggered into the police station and confessed that he pushed his wife out of a tenth-story window.

"Did you kill her?" the sergeant asked.

"I don't think so," he slurred. "That's why I wanna be locked up."

☞ "My wife has a terrible memory," Elroy told his neighbor.

"Forgets everything?" the man asked.

"No," Elroy said. "She remembers."

☞ "I'm sick of the whole thing," the farm wife said to her husband. "You won't work and all you do is mope around the house and bellyache all day. I'm getting a divorce."

"Oh, you don't really mean that," her husband said. "You're just trying to cheer me up."

☞ "We've been married a year and we never quarrel," Elizabeth bragged to her friend. "If a difference of opinion arises and I'm right, my husband gives in."

"But what if he's right?" the friend inquired.

The wife replied, "That hasn't happened yet."

☞ "I took a honeydew vacation this year," the young farmer said. "You know, that's where you stay at home and your wife keeps saying, 'Honey, do this' or 'Honey, do that.'"

☞ "You poor dear, it's too bad he's gone," Bertha said as she consoled the widow of a man who drowned. "I hope you were left something."

"Oh, I was!" the widow assured her. "He left me $50,000."

"Fifty thousand!" said Bertha. "Imagine that! And he couldn't even read or write."

The widow nodded and said, "Or swim."

☞ There was a guy at the hunting shack last deer season who maintained he wasn't henpecked. But he couldn't join in any of the poker games. He said he left all his change at home in his apron pocket.

☛ "Dad, I've got my first part in a school play," the farm boy reported. "I play the part of a man who has been married for 20 years."

"That's a good start," encouraged his father. "Maybe one of these days you'll get a speaking part."

☛ Two old mountaineers came down from the hills and met in town. "How're things at home?" asked one.

"Well, my wife ain't talkin' to me this morning, and I ain't in the mood to interrupt her."

☛ A newly-widowed farm woman told the funeral director proudly, "We were married 30 years and didn't have a single argument all that time."

The mortician replied, "Truly remarkable! What was your secret?"

The widow answered, "No secret. I outweighed him by 50 pounds and he was chicken."

☛ A Kentucky farm couple always showed up together at the farm meetings. The husband, Sam, was a very heavy tobacco chewer, and was never seen without a little trickle of tobacco juice running down the side of his mouth and chin.

Sam was definitely an eyesore, and people couldn't understand how his beautiful, loving wife Roseanne had put up with him all those years.

One day one of the farm ladies asked, "How can you stand all that tobacco juice? It's disgusting. Why don't you leave him?"

"I'd have walked out long ago," Roseanne admitted, "but I certainly couldn't bear the thought of kissing him goodbye."

☛ The list of prizewinners at the county fair was released as follows. "Mrs. Smith won the ladies' rolling pin-throwing contest by hurling a pin 75 feet. Mr. Smith won the 100-yard dash."

☛ A refugee couple arrived in the United States. Finally, after all the red tape and years of study, they were finally made citizens. One day, the husband rushed into the kitchen with the long-awaited news. "Anna! Anna!" he shouted. "At last, we're now official Americans! Now we can live like everyone else does!"

"Fine," replied the wife. "Now you wash the dishes."

☞ Arnold was near the end of his life. As he rested, he decided it was time to call his children to his side. They stood around his bed, waiting for him to speak.

"Children, your mother and I have been married for more than 50 years," Arnold said, "but you should know she made my life miserable. She was a real bad apple. It was a terrible life I had."

One of the sons was shocked at hearing this news and wanted to know why he stayed married to her if everything was as bad as he insisted.

"Because she could bake and cook like an angel," Arnold said. "Even now, I can smell a good strudel baking. Sarah, be a good girl and go get your dying father a piece of strudel."

Arnold closed his eyes and waited for Sarah to return. When he heard her come into the room, he opened his eyes.

"Sarah, where's the strudel?" Arnold asked.

"Mom says you can't have any," Sarah said.

"Why not?"

"She says it's for the funeral tomorrow," the girl answered.

☞ "My wife," said Bob, "talks to herself."

"So does mine," confided Toby, "but she doesn't know it—she thinks I listen."

☞ A grim-faced fellow took a seat at the bar and growled, "Gimme a double."

The guy next to him asked, "Why are you so upset?"

The fellow answered, "Because I just had words with my wife and she moved out."

A guy sitting at the end of the bar looked up from his drink and said, "Do you remember exactly what those words were?"

Chapter 24

Back Stair Stories

"Husbands are like fires.
They go out if unattended."

—Zsa Zsa Gabor

☛ An actor, who had a habit of embellishing his speech with fancy phrases, returned home early one afternoon to surprise his wife. The maid met him in the hall and asked him if he was looking for his wife.

"Yes," he replied in fancy tones, "I seek my dearest friend and severest critic."

"Well," she answered wryly, "your severest critic is in the bedroom and your best friend just jumped out the window."

☛ Pete was at the shop telling how he caught his wife with another man. Both wife and lover were shot.

Everyone was stunned and silent, but then Pete said, "Yeah, but it could've been worse."

"What do you mean by that?" someone said. "What could be worse than a double murder?"

"It could've been the day before," said Pete. "Then he would have shot me."

☛ A midwestern farmer got a phone call in the middle of the night. He picked up the phone, listened, and said, "How should I know? That's 700 miles from here!"

"What was that all about?" his wife said, rolling over.

"I don't know," he said. "Some idiot wanted to know if the coast was clear."

☛ Betty said to her farm husband, "Let's go out tonight and have some fun."

"OK," he answered, "but if you get home first, leave the porch light on."

☛ Wives are like baseball umpires—they make quick decisions, never reverse themselves, and they don't think you're safe when you're out.

☛ The farm couple was sitting on their porch swing when the wife said teasingly, "If I died, would you remarry?"

He scratched his head and said, "Yes, I think I would."

This didn't exactly sit well with his wife, who said in a high voice, "Well, if you remarried, would you give her the sterling silver set we got for a wedding gift?"

The husband again scratched his head, hesitated and said, "Yes, I think I would."

The wife was burning by now and barely spit out the words, "Well, if you remarried, would you give this woman the fur coat you gave me for our last anniversary?"

He moved his feet, scratched his head, and twisted, but said, "Yes, I think I would."

Now the raging wife yelled, "Well, what about my golf clubs. Would you give them to her?"

The husband looked up at his wife and said, "No, I wouldn't give her your golf clubs."

The wife, mad but a little relieved, asked, "Why not my golf clubs? If you're going to give her my sterling silver set, and you're going to give her my fur coat, why not my golf clubs?"

He meekly replied, "Because she's left-handed."

☛ Two hired hands were talking out in the fields. One said, "Man, I've got a girdle on that's killing me."

"Since when have you been wearing a girdle?" the other asked.

He replied, "Ever since my wife found it in the glove compartment."

☛ "I came home, your honor," the upset husband explained, "and found my wife in the arms of a strange man."

The judge said, "And what did she say when you caught her?"

"That's the part that hurt the most, your honor," he said. "She turned and saw me and yelled, 'Well, look who's here! Old Blabbermouth. Now the whole town will know.'"

☛ Jean said to her neighbor, "How can I cure Sam from staying out so late at night?"

"The next time he comes home late," the neighbor said, "call out, 'Is that you, Harry?'"

☞ Coming home from the cattle sale early, the farmer found his wife lying naked in bed, breathing heavily and clearly distracted.

"Alice, what's the matter?" he asked.

"I think I'm having a heart attack," she gasped.

Quickly, he rushed downstairs to the phone and was dialing a doctor when his son hurried in and exclaimed, "Daddy! There's a naked man in the front closet."

Going over to the closet, the farmer opened the door and found his best friend cowering there. "For God's sake, Clyde," blustered the husband, "my wife is upstairs having a heart attack and here you are sneaking around scaring the children."

☞ "So you met your wife at a dance; isn't that romantic," the woman said to the farmer at the doctor's office.

"No, it was embarrassing," he said. "I thought she was at home taking care of the kids."

☞ Marriage is like sitting in a bathtub. After you get used to it, it ain't so hot.

☞ A very successful cattle rancher called home one day with instructions for his wife. When the maid answered, she told him that his wife could not come to the phone at the moment. "Tell her she has to," he demanded. "It's very important. Right now!"

"I'm sorry, sir, but she can't," the maid said. "She's busy."

After he demanded she tell him what's going on, the maid finally said, "Well, sir, she's in the bedroom with Dr. Smith."

"Dr. Smith!" he yelled. "Why, that...listen, I'll tell you what to do. Get a chair, go to the hall closet, and in the back right corner of the top shelf, you'll find a loaded pistol. Take it, and shoot that dog! I'm going to wait right here on the phone until you do it and come back and tell me that you've done it. Got that?"

"Yes, sir," replied the maid. The rancher waited on the phone, and after a while he heard a distant bang. The maid returned and said, "All right, sir, I did it. Now what should I do?"

"Get a kleenex and wipe all the fingerprints off the gun," he instructed. "Then take it out behind the house and throw it as far as you can into the pond in back. Got that?"

There was a pause, and then the maid said, "But there is no pond in the back of the house."

"Oh, my God!" he said. "Isn't this 782-4333?"

☞ A wife caught her husband smiling as he read the card from a fortune-telling machine at the county fair.

Grabbing the card from his hand, she snapped, "So, 'you're going to have a beautiful and charming wife,' are you? Not while I'm alive, Buster, not while I'm alive!"

☞ Entering an oasis, a caravan leader found a sheik sitting beneath a date palm weeping heavily. "What's the matter?" the caravan leader asked.

The sheik moaned, "One of my wives stole my horse, rode off in the desert and eloped with my worst enemy."

"Tsk, tsk!" the nomad exclaimed with sympathy. "Was it your favorite wife?"

"No," sobbed the sheik. "But it was my favorite horse."

☞ A man in town heard about the wife of a farm machinery dealer who was putting a limousine up for sale at a ridiculously low price. When he arrived at the house, he asked, "What's wrong with the car?"

"Nothing," she said. "If you want it for $20, give me the twenty and take it away. If you don't want it, please don't waste my time."

He asked for the keys and went to the garage, backed the car out and handed her the $20 bill. "Now, you have your money, so what's the catch?"

"There isn't any," she said. "My husband just died and in his will he instructed that the Cadillac be sold and the proceeds be given to his secretary."

☞ A farmer stopped for a quick beer after picking up a load of feed and happened to notice an old girlfriend across the bar. He went over and renewed the acquaintance. One beer turned into several cocktails, followed by dinner. When he finally looked at the clock it was close to midnight.

"Your wife is going to be furious," the woman said.

"I'll handle her," the farmer replied as he asked the waitress for the piece of chalk she was using to mark up the next day's specials.

He rubbed the chalk on his hands and his trousers and bid his old flame, as surprised as she was, goodnight.

His wife was waiting at the door with the question, "Where have you been?"

"Well, honey, it's like this," he answered. "I stopped for a quick beer and ran into an old girlfriend. We had some drinks and dinner, and I just lost track of the time."

The wife then noticed the chalk on his hands and trousers.

"You're lying!" she said. "You were with those no-good, dead-beat bowling buddies of yours again."

☞ "Boy, am I scared," said the small-town Romeo to his barber. "I got a letter today from a man saying he'd shoot me if I didn't stay away from his wife."

"Well, that's not so bad," the barber answered. "All you have to do is stay away from her."

The worried man replied, "Yeah, I know, but he didn't sign his name."

☞ Two farm wives were gossiping. The first said, "What I say, is that if you give a man enough rope, he'll hang himself."

"Oh, I don't agree," the other woman answered. "I gave my husband enough rope and he skipped."

☞ "Who is the Ethel you talked about in your sleep last night?" a farm wife asked her husband at the breakfast table.

"Oh," he said, "That's just a horse that me and the guys bet on at the track."

"Well," said the wife, "your horse called today and said you left your socks at her place."

☞ The small town fire siren blew and the engine went roaring by the corner tavern. Joe put his beer down on the bar and said, "There goes the volunteer fire department. I'd better get moving."

"I didn't know you were a volunteer fireman," the bartender said.

"I'm not," said Joe. "My girlfriend's husband is."

☞ Because he suspected his wife was cheating on him, Vince left work early to check on her. When he arrived at their apartment on the 17th floor, he saw his wife running up and down the halls half-naked, all excited.

So jealous Vince grabbed his gun. The first person he saw walking down the hall was the milkman, so he shot him dead. Then he ran over to the window and saw a man hurrying along, so he grabbed the refrigerator and tossed it out the window, killing the man on the street.

Later, at the Pearly Gates, three men went before St. Peter. St. Peter asked what happened, and the milkman replied, "I was just delivering milk when this guy shot me."

He then asked the guy from the street what happened. "I

was late for an appointment, so I was hurrying along when somebody threw a refrigerator out the window and it killed me," he said.

Then St. Peter asked the third guy how he fit into the story. "You won't believe this," he said, "but I was just sitting in the refrigerator..."

☞ There's a fellow in town who has been married for 25 years and has never stopped being romantic. Of course, his wife will break his neck if she ever finds out about it.

☞ A couple was sitting at a restaurant table enjoying cocktails. Suddenly, the waiter ran to the table. "Madam," the waiter exclaimed, "your husband just slid under the table!"

"No," the lady said, "my husband just walked in the door!"

☞ Dusty was at the university ag conference and finished up a day earlier than expected so he sent a wire to his wife that he would be home a day early. When he walked into his house he found his wife in the arms of another man. Furious, he picked up his bag and stormed out.

On the way, he ran into his mother-in-law coming up the walk, told her what happened and said he was filing for divorce.

"Give my daughter a chance to explain before you do anything rash," the mother-in-law pleaded.

"Let her explain to you," Dusty grumbled. "I'm going to the bar."

About an hour later the mother-in-law phoned the bar. "Dusty, I knew my daughter would have a logical explanation," she said. "She didn't receive your telegram."

☞ "Will there be anything else, sir?" the bellhop asked after dropping the couple's bags off in the luxury suite.

"I don't think so," the man said.

"Anything for your wife?" the bellhop asked.

"Oh, yes," he said. "Would you please bring me a post card that I could mail to her?

☞ Three boy scouts knocked at the door of Barney's house. "We're having a raffle for poor widow Johnson," they said. "Will you buy a ticket?"

"Can't do it, boys," Barney said. "My wife wouldn't let me keep her even if I won."

Children—Our Bundles Of Joy

"I've seen kids ride bicycles, run, play ball, set up a camp, swing, fight a war, swim and race for eight hours...yet have to be driven to the garbage can."

—Erma Bombeck

Chapter 25

All In The Family

"If any of us had a child that we thought was as bad as we know we are, we would have cause to start to worry."
—*Will Rogers*

☛ A mother, pointing to a photo in the local newspaper, said to her little boy, "These little boys are orphans. They have no mother or father or even an Aunt Gertrude. Would you like to give them something?"
"Yes," the little boy replied. "Let's give them Aunt Gertrude."

☛ On their first vacation at the lake, a farmer's son wandered back to his dad dragging the top half of a bikini bathing suit along the edge of the beach. The farmer said, "Now, son, show Daddy exactly where you found that."

☛ The kindergarten teacher asked a new arrival what her father's name was.
"Daddy," replied the little girl.
"No, I mean his first name—what does your mother call him?"
"She doesn't call him anything," the girl answered, confused. "She likes him."

☛ The farm mother was reading the newspaper on her steps when she saw her oldest son was up to mischief. "Peter," she yelled, "get your little brother's hat out of that mud puddle!"
Peter turned and hollered, "I can't, Mom. It's strapped too tight under his chin."

☛ "Who taught you that dreadful word?" Johnny's mother asked after the youngster blurted out a walloping curse.

"The Easter Bunny," Johnny answered.

"The Easter Bunny?"

"Yes, Mama," he said. "Last year when he fell over the chair in the hall on his way downstairs with the eggs."

☛ Three little boys were talking at recess about how tough they were. The first boy said, "I'm so tough I wear out a pair of shoes every week!"

The second boy boasted, "Why, that's nothing. I wear out a pair of blue jeans every day."

"You guys aren't so tough," piped up the third boy. "I wear out my grandma and grandpa in an hour."

☛ A little girl was talking to her mother before bed. "Is it true, Mom, that God will provide for us?"

"Yes, that's true, Becky," she said.

"Is it true that Santa brings all the toys and goodies?"

"That's true."

"And is it true, Mom," Becky said, "that the stork brings the baby?"

Her mother nodded once again.

"Well," the daughter asked, "would you mind telling me why Daddy is hanging around here?"

☛ One farmer recalls his growing up. "My mother had a large family for religious reasons," he said. "The more kids in our family, the better our chances of winning at bingo."

☛ A mother was lecturing her son on sharing. "Now, Chad, you shouldn't be selfish with your toys," she said. "I've told you to let your younger brother play with them half the time."

"That's what I've been doing," Chad explained. "I take the sled going downhill, and he takes it going uphill."

☛ One summer evening during a particularly violent thunderstorm, a mother was tucking her small boy into bed.

She was about to turn off the light when he asked with a tremor in his voice, "Mommy, will you sleep with me tonight?"

The mother smiled and gave him a reassuring hug. "I can't do that, dear," she explained. "I have to sleep in Daddy's room."

A long silence was broken at last by a shaken voice saying, "The big sissy!"

☛ At school, little Tommy was upset. "What's the matter?" his teacher asked.

"I think my mother wants to get rid of me," he cried.

"That's ridiculous," the teacher said. "Why do you say that?"

"Well," Tommy said, "this morning she wrapped my lunch in a road map."

☛ A nine-year-old Tennessee boy asked his parents, "Where did I come from?"

After consultation with each other, the parents sat their son down and went into the total story, from conception to birth.

The boy found it all interesting but commented, "But what I want to know is, did I come from Memphis or Nashville?"

☛ A definition of a brat: A child who acts like yours, but belongs to the neighbors.

☛ Two farm youngsters were discussing their fathers one afternoon, especially the little quirks in their behavior. One boy asked the other, "Does your daddy have a den?"

"Nope," replied his little friend. "He just growls all over the place at our house."

☛ A father returned home from his usual day of work in the fields and found his small son sitting on the front steps looking mighty unhappy. "What's wrong, son?" he asked.

"Just between you and me," the tear-faced lad replied, "I simply can't get along with your wife."

☛ "Hey, Mom," D.J. said as their train rolled over the tracks. "What was the name of the last station we stopped at?"

His mother answered, "Don't bother me, D.J., I'm reading."

But D.J. persisted. "I thought you'd like to know, Mom," he said, "because little brother got off there."

☛ Three proud mothers were discussing their eight-year-old sons at the 4-H meeting. The first said, "I just know my little Daniel is going to be a mechanical engineer. Every toy he gets, he immediately tears it apart to see what makes it work."

The second mother said, "I'm so proud of my little Freddy. He'll be a fine lawyer for sure. He argues with the other kids all the time."

The third said, "No question about it. My little Harold is destined to be a doctor. He never comes when I call him."

☛ The problems of her future had been weighing heavily on five-year-old June's mind. She decided to consult her mother.

"If I get married someday," she asked, "will I have a husband like Papa?"

"Yes, dear," her mother said.

"And if I don't get married will I be an old maid like Aunt Susan?"

"Yes."

"Well," June murmured to herself, "I sure am in a fix."

☛ The parents of an eight-year-old boy who was away at 4-H Camp for the first time hadn't heard from him, so they called him and were a bit disappointed to discover he hadn't missed them at all.

"Have any of the other kids gotten homesick?" his mother asked.

"Only the ones who have dogs," replied the boy.

☛ Young Timmy walked up to his dad as he worked on the tractor and said, "Daddy, if you give me a quarter, I'll tell you what the bread man said to Mama this morning."

His father flipped him a quarter and demanded, "What did that @#*&%#$@ say?"

Timmy answered, "He said, 'Any bread today, Lady?'"

☛ "I'm really worried," said one little boy to a friend. "Dad slaves away on the farm so I'll never want for anything, so I'll be able to go to the university if I want to. Mom works hard washing and ironing, cleaning up after me and taking care of me when I get sick. They spend every day of their lives working just on my behalf. I'm worried."

"What have you got to worry about then?"

The boy replied, "I'm afraid they might try to escape."

☛ Paul told his wife before she met the family for the first time, "As a child, my older brother was always hungry. You know how some kids make model airplanes? Well, he made model hamburgers."

☞ A small boy rushed into the local drugstore. "Quick, quick," he screamed, "my pop is hanging by his pants leg from a barbed wire fence!"

"What do you need?" asked the druggist. "Is he hurt, or do you need help getting him down?"

"No, no," shouted the youngster. "Just gimme another roll of film for my camera."

☞ A family who had been living in very cramped quarters finally moved into their new, larger home. A neighbor asked the eight-year-old son how he liked his new house.

He replied, "Oh, we like it fine! My two sisters and I each have our own rooms now. But poor Mom, she's still stuck in the same bedroom with Dad."

☞ As the farmer finished his chores and decided to call it a day, he found his three-year-old crying in the front yard. "What's wrong?" he asked his son.

"Mama ran over my tricycle," he sobbed.

"Bobby, if I've told you once, I've told you a thousand times—don't leave your trike on the porch."

☞ After Kelly ran in the house, bent over and crying, her mother asked, "Mike, why did you kick your little sister in the stomach?"

"Well," Mike explained, "she turned around."

☞ "Don't eat so much," said the father to his younger spitting image. "You're making a pig out of yourself. Do you know what a pig is?"

"Yes, Daddy," replied the toddler. "It's a hog's little son."

☞ A farmer's daughter was practicing her singing for the school pageant. Her dad came home from the fields early.

"What's that queer noise?" he asked.

"That, dear," replied his wife proudly, "is Jean, cultivating her voice."

"Ah," the farmer said, "that's not cultivating, that's harrowing."

☞ A farmer had to go to the big city and decided to take his little daughter with him. When they got to a skyscraper, the elevator doors opened and they walked into the crowded elevator.

132

The elevator stopped at a floor and a woman suddenly turned around, slapped the farmer across the face and walked out in a huff.

As the other people in the elevator gave him dirty looks, the little girl remarked, "I didn't like her either, Daddy. She stepped on my toe, so I pinched her."

☛ A woman who had just given birth to triplets was explaining to a friend that triplets happened only once in 15,000 times.

"My goodness!" exclaimed the friend. "How did you find time to do your housework?"

☛ Look on the bright side of things. There is no child so bad that it can't be used as an income tax deduction.

☛ A little girl was watching her mother spread cold cream on her face. "What's it for, Mommy?" she asked.

"That's to make me beautiful, darling," the mother explained.

She watched her mother remove the cream, and then in a tone of sadness whispered, "It didn't work, did it?"

☛ As Brad got the usual lecture on laziness from his father, his dad said once again, "When I was a boy I thought nothing of a 10-mile walk."

Brad answered, "Well, I don't think so much of it, either."

☛ Max climbed up into his mother's lap and asked, "Mother, are you very poor?"

"Why, no, Max," his mother replied. "I'm very rich. I have you and your brother Bill, and you two are worth millions to me."

Max encountered: "Well, then, Mother, do you think you could mortgage Billy and buy me a new basketball?"

☛ Judy and Jeff were discussing the farm chores their father had just handed out. Judy asked, "Did Dad promise you something for doing the chores?"

Jeff responded, "No, but he promised me something if I didn't."

☛ Two little boys were discussing bathroom scales. One said, "It's just like magic! I just turn this little wheel backwards and all of a sudden Mom becomes a lot easier to get along with."

☛ A mother described to her small son the happy times of her girlhood, when she rode ponies, slid down haystacks, and waded in the brook at the farm.

When the woman finished, the boy sighed and said, "Gee, Mom, I wish I'd met you earlier."

☛ A man pushing a cart containing a screaming baby through a large supermarket was overheard by the patrons as he softly repeated two phrases, "Keep calm, boy," and "Don't get excited, Tony."

A lady remarked as she pushed her cart next to his, "My goodness, it's nice of you to do the family shopping and mind the little baby at the same time, but don't you think you could do more for little Tony than comfort him with those phrases?"

"Lady," replied the harried man, "I'm Tony."

☛ At the dinner table, the mother asked Phillip about her husband's accident earlier in the day. "What did your father say when he fell out of the silo?"

Phillip asked, "Shall I leave out all the naughty words?"

"Of course!"

Phillip thought for a second and then said, "Nothing!"

☛ The young boy and his mother, looking at the family album, came to a picture of a handsome young man with dark, wavy hair.

"Who's that?" asked the boy.

"Why, that's your father," the mother said proudly.

"Well," the boy said skeptically, "then who's that bald-headed guy who's living with us?"

☛ A nine-year-old farm girl, accompanied by her younger brother, stopped an elderly man on the street and said, "Please, mister, for 50 cents I'll have my brother imitate a hen for you."

Amusingly handing her two quarters, he asked, "And how does he do that, my little woman? Cackle?"

"No, sir," the girl said. "None of those cheap imitations. I'll make him eat a worm."

Chapter 26

Here Comes Trouble

"There's not a man in America who at one time or another hasn't had a secret desire to boot a child in the rear."

—*W.C. Fields*

☛ Two farm kids were sent to their rooms with the warning that they had better act more like adults. "What do you suppose all that adult stuff means?" Darren asked.

"Gosh," said David, "I don't know."

They began to think. Finally, one perked up.

"Mom swears sometimes," Darren said. "I heard her say %&@#)%!"

"You think that's the adult stuff?"

"Could be."

"Yeah, you might be right," David said. "Remember when Dad called Mr. Jones across the street a #$%&@#$%$@#%?"

The next morning at breakfast, the youngsters were asked what kind of cereal they wanted.

"I'll have some of those %@#)%! corn flakes," Darren said.

He quickly got a whack on the ear that sent him flying across the room.

"How about you?" Dad asked David. "I don't know," he said, "but you can bet your #$%&@#$%$$@#% I don't want any of those %@#)% cornflakes."

☛ A small farm boy had been caught being naughty. After his mother told him he was going to get a whipping, he fled upstairs and hid in a far corner under the bed.

When the father came into the house from the field, the mother told him what happened. He went upstairs and proceeded to crawl under the bed toward the youngster.

Excitedly, the boy whispered, "Hello, Pop, is she after you, too?"

☞ The farmer and his small son got in a crowded elevator. A plump lady turned to the father and said, "Aren't you afraid he'll be squashed?"

"Not at all," the farmer said, "he bites."

☞ Sarah and Suzie were playing house in their mother's bedroom when Suzie accidentally broke the mirror over the dressing table.

"You're going to have seven years of bad luck," Sarah said.

"I'm not worried about the next seven years," Suzie said. "I'm just worried about the next seven minutes."

☞ The traveling salesman knocked at the door of a farm home. As the door was flung open a nine-year-old puffing on a long, black cigar appeared. Trying to cover his amazement, the salesman said, "Good morning, sonny. Is your mother in?"

The boy removed the cigar from his mouth, flicked off its ashes and replied, "What do YOU think?"

☞ A farmer was punishing his young son for pushing the outhouse into the creek.

"But, gee," said the boy, "whaddya want to punish me for? After all, you asked me who did it and I told the truth. When George Washington chopped down the cherry tree and told his father the truth, he didn't get punished."

"That's so," said the farmer with a wry look on his face. "But when George cut down the cherry tree, his father wasn't sitting in it!"

☞ A little farm boy was being led out to the woodshed after cutting off his sister's hair. As his father dragged him by the collar, he asked, "Dad, did Grandpa spank you when you were a little boy?"

"Yes," his father answered.

"And did Great-Grandpa spank Grandpa when he was a little boy?" he asked.

"Yes."

"Well," the boy said seriously, "don't you think with my help you could overcome this inherited sadism?"

☞ Nick had acquired the habit of using profane language quite extensively. He was warned by his mother never to say such words again, or she would pack his clothes and turn him out.

Nick promised his mother that he wouldn't, but it wasn't long before she heard him swear. She immediately packed his clothes and put him out of the house.

The boy stood on the steps for approximately an hour, and his mother, who was watching from the window, finally opened the door. "Why didn't you leave?" she asked, expecting him to say he'd stopped swearing for good.

"I was wondering," Nick replied, "where the *#?!&%@#$# would I go?"

☛ Little Stevie walked in from school and threw his books on the table. "What did Mama's little baby learn in school today?" asked his mother.

"I learned two punks not to call me Mama's little baby," he said.

☛ Steaming mad, the farmer rushed into the kitchen and hollered, "Whose fingerprints are those on the door I just painted?"

The youngest son spoke up: "Not mine—I always kick the door open when I come in the house."

☛ Two men were sitting around talking about their child-hood days. "My father was a cultured man," said the first. "Every time he took me to the wood shed he proposed a toast."

"Really? What was it?"

"Bottoms up," he said.

☛ "Russell, when that naughty boy threw stones at you, why didn't you come and tell me instead of throwing them back at him?" his mother asked.

"What good would that do, Mom?" snorted Russell. "You can't hit the side of a barn."

☛ When a farmer had to go into town to pick up some supplies, he decided to take his little boy along to see Santa. When the boy hopped up into Santa's lap, he presented him with a list of requests—a bicycle, a train, a bat and ball, a rocket set, an airplane and an astronaut suit.

"Thanks for the list," Santa said. "I'll check between now and Christmas to see whether or not you've been a good boy."

"Never mind checking," the little boy said. "I'll settle right now for the bicycle."

☛ Little Dennis came home crying to his mother that the neighbor boy had hit him. "Did you hit him back?" she asked. "No," Dennis said, "I hit him first."

☛ A little boy came up to his mother and said, "Say, Mom, do you remember that antique flower pot that's been handed down from generation to generation?"
"Of course, dear," said his mother.
"Well, this generation just dropped it!"

☛ A little boy was playing in the sand at the park when a big bully came along and beat him up. He told the little girl next to him, "That was karate, from Japan."
The next day the big bully again beat up the little kid, leaving the message, "That was judo, from Japan."
The next day, the bully appeared again. But this time, the little boy beat up the bigger boy, and left word with the little girl to tell him, "That was a lug wrench from Western Auto."

☛ What's a small farm boy's definition of conscience? Something that makes you tell your mother before your sister does.

☛ While the two boys were walking around at the county fair, they stumbled across the gypsy fortune-telling booths. "Do you really think anyone can tell the future with cards?" one boy asked.
"My mother can," the other boy answered. "She took one look at my report card and told me exactly what was going to happen when Dad got home."

☛ "I'm ashamed of you, Robert," said the farmer when his young son came into the house. "I saw you kick your friend. Why did you do that?"
"Aw," Robert said. "I was tired of playing with 'im and wanted him to go home."
"Then why didn't you just ask him to go home?" asked his father.
"Why, Daddy," cried Robert in a shocked tone. "That wouldn't have been polite."

☛ Mark asked, "Dad, can we paint the car purple?"
"No," Dad hollered, "Certainly not!"
Paul punched Mark in the arm and said, "See, I told you we should have asked."

138

☛ "Chip," said the teacher, "if you were always kind and polite to your friends, do you know how they'd feel about you?"

Chip said, "Yeah, they'd think I was afraid they could lick me."

☛ Willie had been playing hooky from school and spent the day fishing. On the way home, he met one of his young friends who asked, "Catch anything?"

"Don't know," replied Willie. "I ain't been home yet."

☛ The young farm mother was shocked to learn her little Sammy had told some lies. Taking the lad on her knee, she graphically explained the consequence of lying.

"A tall green man," she began, "with red fiery eyes and two sharp horns grabs little boys who tell lies and carries them off at night. He takes them to Mars where they have to work hard in a dark canyon for 50 years. Now, you won't tell a lie again, will you Sammy?"

"No, ma'am," he replied. "You can tell 'em better than I can."

☛ A small boy asked his mother, "Can I help Dad put on the snow chains? I know all the words."

☛ From the farmhouse kitchen came the sound of broken glass and broken china.

"Peter," cried his mother from the living room, "What on earth are you doing?"

"Nothing right now," Peter said. "It's already done."

☛ Two farm mothers were talking about their children at the weekly bridge club game.

"My three boys stick together," said one mother. "When one of them gets into trouble, neither of the others will tell on him."

"Then how do you find out which one to punish?" the other asked.

"It's easy," she explained. "I send them all to bed without supper. Then the next morning I thrash the one with the black eye."

☛ For several days, six-year-old Kenny had been complaining to his dad that some of the neighborhood's farm children had been picking on him at the bus stop. Deciding it was time to teach Kenny some self-defense, his father showed him how to make a fist and let it fly the next time his rowdy little playmate picked on him.

That afternoon the door burst open and Kenny rushed in, his eyes shining in triumph. "Daddy," he shouted, "I did it! I hit her!"

☛ Two youngsters were dragging a large, awkward sack through the toy department of a local store. They were making a lot of noise and bumping into customers.

The manager came up. "Now, boys," he scolded, "if you keep on being troublesome, Santa Claus won't come to your house."

"That's what you think," retorted on youngster. "Who do you think we got in this sack?"

☛ Little Andy had a problem. It seems he had picked up a collection of four-letter words and his parents weren't having much success curbing his language. One day, Andy was invited to a birthday party and his mother, in no uncertain terms, warned him, "I've talked to Mary's mother and if you use even one swear word, she's going to send you home!"

Off to the party Andy went, but five minutes later he was home again. "What happened?" his mother asked.

Andy looked up and said, "The damn party's tomorrow."

Chapter 27

Cookie Jar Blues

*"Insanity is hereditary. You
can get it from your children."*

—*Sam Levenson*

☛ Three schoolboys were waiting in the doctor's office for their shots, reading magazines as they awaited the doctor's needle.

The doctor went up to the first one who was reading *Popular Mechanics* and said, "Jimmy, what are you going to be when you grow up?"

Immediately Jimmy said, "I'm going to be a mechanic. I want to fix autos and make airplanes fly."

He then went up to Tommy who was reading *Field and Stream.*

"Tommy, what are you going to be?"

Tommy, without hesitation, said, "I want to be a hunting and fishing guide. Yes, that's what I want to be."

The doctor then went over to little red-headed, freckle-faced Joey who was carefully examining *Playboy.*

When asked the same question, Joey thought for a moment and then said slowly, "I don't know what you call it, but I can hardly wait to get started."

☛ A woman and her young boy boarded the train and took their seats. Seated directly across from them, a man stared at them and finally said, "I can't believe how ugly your kid is."

Upset, the mother turned the other way. A drunk got on and sat next to her and hollered, "Wow! Your kid sure is hideous!"

The mother got up and complained to the conductor, who said he'd look into the situation. He returned a few moments later and said, "We apologize. Please go to the dining car for a free meal on us...and ask the waiter for a free banana for your monkey, too."

☛ One night a father of 10 was to keep watch over the brood while his wife went to a meeting. Before leaving, she instructed him not to let a single child come downstairs.

He had just settled down with a farm magazine when he heard steps on the stairway. "Get back up those stairs!" he yelled authoritatively.

A few minutes later, he heard steps again on the stairs. "Get back up those steps or I'll spank you!" he barked.

Five or 10 minutes passed and he heard steps again. He dashed to the stairs to see a couple of tiny feet disappear at the top of the stairs.

He had hardly sat down with his book again when a neighbor lady came to the front door. "Oh, Mr. Jones, I can't find my little Billy anywhere. Have you seen him?"

"Here I am, Mom," wailed a tearful voice from the top of the stairs. "He won't let me come home!"

☛ During the middle of Sunday School class, little Leonard raised his hand and said, "I've got to go to the bathroom."

The teacher told him to go right ahead and she continued with the lecture. Leonard came back and said he couldn't find it, so she gave him clear instructions.

A few moments later, Leonard came back and said shyly, "I can't find it." The teacher sent an older boy to help Leonard, who returned shortly after leaving.

"We found it," the boy said. "He had his pants on backwards."

☛ A stranger saw a little farm girl playing in front of her house and asked, "What's the name of your kitten?"

She said, "BenHur."

"That's a funny name for a cat," the man said.

The girl answered, "We called him Ben until he had kittens."

☛ Katie and Michelle were walking through the big city museum and stopped in front of an Egyptian mummy case. The label read: "2453 B.C."

Katie whispered, "What does 2453 B.C. mean?"

"I don't know," Michelle said. "Maybe the license on the car that hit him."

☛ One three-year-old's explanation of being atop a ladder, eating cookies, "I just climbed up here to smell them and my tooth got caught!"

☛ "Mom," said little Nancy, "can I have a quarter for the poor old man who is standing in front of the house crying?"

"Yes," said her mother. "Here's the quarter. Go give it to him. But, what is he crying about?"

As Nancy sprinted across the street she said, "He's crying, 'Peanuts, 25 cents a bag.'"

☛ The little city girl questioned her father, "How many kinds of milk are there?"

"Why, there's condensed milk, evaporated milk and—but why do you ask?"

"Well," she said, "I was drawing a picture of a cow and I want to know how many faucets to put on her."

☛ Mother walked out to the barn and found Luke shaking and scolding his pet rabbit impatiently. "Come on now, tell me what's 5 and 5?"

"Whatever are you doing, Luke?" the mother demanded.

"Well," Luke explained, "teacher said rabbits could multiply rapidly and my dumb bunny can't even add."

☛ An elderly woman was escorting two little farm girls around the zoo. While they were looking at the stork, she told them the legend of the ungainly bird and how it was instrumental in bringing them to their mothers.

The children looked at each other in astonishment and one whispered to the other, "Don't you think maybe we better tell this old woman the truth?"

☛ "Mother," asked a curious Freddie, "is it true an apple a day keeps the doctor away?"

"So I understand, Freddie, but why do you ask?"

He replied, "Well, I've kept away 13 doctors this morning, but I'm afraid one will have to come this afternoon."

☛ There was a mother who made an urgent call to her son's 4-H Club camp in the backwoods within minutes after she read a letter from her son, who wrote: "I'm still a lousy swimmer, so I go down to the lake alone and practice after dark."

☛ The second-grade teacher strained to help a pupil don his galoshes. After five minutes of grunting and struggling to fasten the eight buckles on the boots, the boy panted, "The reason they were so hard to get on is because they're not mine."

In despair, the teacher struggled to get them off again. Just as soon as they were off, the boy said, "They're my sister's but Mommy makes me wear them because I don't have any."

☛ A farmer, going to the city for a beef producers meeting, decided to take his young son with him. They went together to the opera and the son watched as the conductor started waving his baton and the soprano began her aria.

The boy watched everything intently and finally asked, "Why is he hitting her with his stick?"

"He's not hitting her," said the farmer with a chuckle.

"Well, then," asked the boy, "why is she screaming?"

☛ The third-grade teacher was giving her pupils a lesson on problem solving. "Now try to picture this scene. A man is on the riverbank, slips and falls into the river. While he is thrashing about in the water, his wife, hearing his screams and knowing he cannot swim, rushes to the bank! Now, why does she rush to the bank?"

From the rear of the room, a little boy replied, "To draw out his insurance money?"

☛ A country preacher noticed a group of boys standing around a small stray dog. "What are you boys up to?" he asked.

"Telling lies," said one of the boys. "The one who tells the biggest lie gets the dog."

"Why, when I was your age," the shocked minister said, "I never even thought of telling a lie."

A bit crestfallen, the boys stared at one another. Finally, one of them shrugged and said, "I guess he wins the dog."

☛ "Well, Jeffrey, how did you get along in school today?" his mother asked.

"OK, Mom, but that new teacher is always asking us some dumb questions," Jeffrey said. "Today she asked everybody where they were born."

The mother inquired, "Did you tell her that you were born in the Women's Hospital?"

The son replied, "No. I didn't want the whole class to think I was a sissy. I told her Memorial Stadium."

☛ A woman walked up to a six-year-old boy who was puffing away on a cigarette. "Does your mother know you smoke?" she asked as she reached for the cigarette.

"Lady," the kid said, turning away. "Does your husband know you stop and talk to strange men on the street?"

☛ A nursery school teacher was delivering a station wagon full of kids home one day when a fire truck zoomed past. Sitting on the front seat was a Dalmatian dog. The children fell to discussing the dog's duties.

"They use him to keep the crowds back," said one youngster.

"No," said another, "he's just for good luck."

A third child brought the argument to a close. "They use the dog," he said firmly, "to find the fire hydrant."

☛ Eight-year-old Danny was being taught the proper way to ask a girl for a dance by the teacher in a dance instruction class.

A half hour later, Danny walked up to the teacher and asked, "Now, how do you get rid of her?"

☛ Keith surprised his parents at bedtime when he said during his prayers: "Please bless my mother, my father, and make Chicago the capital of the United States."

His father said, "Why do you want Chicago to be the capital of the United States?"

"That's what I put on my test paper," Keith said.

☛ A neighbor boy knocked at the door. "Can Timmy come out and play with me?" he asked.

"I'm sorry, but Timmy is taking his nap," the mother replied.

"Then can Timmy's new bike come out and play?" he inquired hopefully.

☛ A middle-aged farmer was talking to Ralph, the next-door neighbor's boy. The farmer asked, "Ralph, what are you going to do when you grow up and become a big man like me?"

Ralph took a long look and said, "Diet."

☛ The wife of an old farmer had just become a mother for the 17th time. The ever-growing family seemed to be a major concern to an inquisitive eight-year-old boy in the family.

One day, lolling idly in the field, he spotted an airplane, the first he'd ever seen. As he watched, several men parachuted out.

He ran home, grabbed his father, and said, "Get your gun and come a'running, Pa! The stork just flew over and he's dropping 'em full-grown now!"

☛ Some youngsters around the farm were playing Wild West. One of the more enterprising kids had dragged out an old packing box, made a bar out of it and scrawled a sign which read, "This is the Wild West and this is the Last Chance Saloon."

Another kid ran up, pounded on the box and said, "Waaal, I'll have myself a rye."

A third young boy, much younger and apparently less sophisticated, staggered up alongside him and squeaked, "I'll have a whole wheat."

☛ A housewife heard a loud knock on her door, opened it and there stood two boys. One of them was holding a list in his hands.

"Lady," he said, "me and my brother are on a treasure hunt. Do you have three grains of wheat, a sheet of toilet paper and a dodo bird skeleton?"

She replied, "Sorry, I'm fresh out. That's a hard list. What treasure hunt is this?"

"Well," said the boy, "if we find everything on this list, we each win $5."

"And who is going to give you the money?" she asked.

"Our babysitter's boyfriend."

☛ A farm mother was listening to little Todd saying his prayers, while Granny sat knitting. Toward the end of his prayers, his mother was surprised to hear her little son raise his voice and positively roar: "And please, can I have a bicycle for my birthday?"

"But Todd," she protested, "God isn't deaf."

"No," answered the little boy seriously, "but Granny is!"

Chapter 28

Out Of The Mouths Of Babes

"Thank God kids never mean well."

—*Lily Tomlin*

☛ One blistering hot day when they had guests for dinner, Mom asked four-year-old Johnny to say grace. "But I don't know what to say," the boy explained.

"Oh, just say what you hear me say," the mother replied.

Johnny bowed his head obediently and murmured, "O, Lord, why did I invite all these people over here on a hot day like this?"

☛ A farm mother was preparing an early supper so her 11-year-old daughter could get to the 4-H meeting on time. Everything was ready when she discovered she was almost out of ketchup.

She was thumping away at the end of the nearly-empty bottle when the phone rang. "Would you get that for me?" she called.

The daughter obliged and the caller said she was from the PTA and wished to speak to her mother. She said, "My mother can't come to the phone right now. She's hitting the bottle!"

☛ A boring, long-winded relative visited her nephew and his family, staying throughout the day. When at last she started to leave, she asked her nephew's small son, "Well, Donny, are you going to walk me to the bus stop?"

He replied, "I can't ma'am. As soon as you leave, we're going to eat!"

☛ A young farm mother brought her son to the doctor's office for an examination. Concerned that perhaps the boy didn't get enough sleep, the doctor asked, "What time does the sandman come to your house?"

"Right after Dad goes bowling," the youngster replied.

☞ A small farm girl was lost in a department store and was crying loudly when a clerk asked him what was the matter.

"I'm lost," the little girl said.

"Oh," said the clerk. "Who were you with?"

"My father."

"And what's your father like?" the clerk inquired.

"Beer and women," said the sobbing girl.

☞ A mother was overheard yelling at her son, "I don't care if the basement wall is cracking. Stop telling everyone you come from a broken home!"

☞ After hearing the grown-ups discuss the opposite sex, a small boy turned to the neighbor girl and asked, "Are you the opposite sex, or am I?"

☞ Little Susie had just returned from a birthday party and was brought into the living room by her mother to be exhibited before the bridge club.

"Tell the nice ladies what you did at the party," urged the doting mother.

"I ate too much cake and threw up," Susie said.

☞ A farm mother said to her sick boy, "I think your new nurse is very nice, Stevie. Do you like her?"

Stevie replied, "No, Mama, I hate her. I'd like to grab her by the hair and bite her on the neck like Daddy does."

☞ "I am really glad you came," little Todd said to a family guest. "Now Dad can do the trick he said he'd do."

"And what might that be?" asked the lady sweetly.

"Well," said Todd, "he said that if you showed up today he'd climb the wall."

☞ The small daughter of a newly-elected town mayor was quite proud of her father's accomplishment and was always introducing herself as "Mayor Wilson's daughter."

Her mother, thinking it sounded rather snobbish, instructed the girl to refer to herself simply as Betty Wilson.

That afternoon, Betty was playing in her front yard when a lady came by and gushed, "My goodness, you're Mayor Wilson's daughter, aren't you?"

"I thought I was," replied the little girl, "but Mama says no."

☞ About the only things children will share willingly are communicable diseases and their mother's age.

☞ During the children's field trip to the zoo, the teacher pointed to a deer and asked Frankie to name the animal. When he didn't answer, she said, "Here's a hint—what does your mama call your daddy?"

"You mean," shrieked the boy, "that's a lummox?"

☞ A four-year-old farm boy was walking through the grocery store when his mother noticed he was sucking his thumb. She said, "See that fat man in the next aisle? If you don't stop sucking your thumb, you'll be just like him."

Wandering around the store, the little boy spied a pregnant lady and went up to her and said, "Pardon me, lady. I don't know your name but I know what you've been doing."

☞ Children seldom misquote you. They repeat word for word exactly what you shouldn't have said.

☞ The entire family clan gathered to honor Grandma on her birthday, but she wasn't telling anyone her age. It was a big question mark until her grandson walked in front of the crowd of relatives and piped up, "She's 74 years old."

She grabbed her grandson playfully and asked, "How did you know my age?"

"I sneaked into your purse and looked at your driver's license," he explained. "And you know something—I found out something that must've made Grandpa very angry. It says on your license that you got an 'F' in sex."

☞ Two visitors in a farm home were sitting alone when the hostess' four-year-old girl walked in on them. They looked her over very carefully, then one spelled to the other, "She's not very p-r-e-t-t-y, is she?"

Before the other woman had a chance to respond, the little girl said, "No, I'm not, but I'm awfully i-n-t-e-l-l-i-g-e-n-t."

☛ There was a young farm girl who had developed the habit of getting out of her own bed and crawling in with Mom and Dad whenever she had a bad dream or felt lonely.

After it started to happen on a regular basis, they decided to discourage it and frequently carted a sobbing little body back to her own bed.

When her dad had to go out of town for a few days to a Farm Progress convention, he instructed his wife, "Now don't give in while I'm gone and ruin the progress we've made."

Upon his return, his wife and daughter met him at the airport. The little girl had a grin a mile wide as she saw her father and started running toward him through the crowd of passengers.

When she got within earshot, she yelled excitedly, "Daddy, Daddy! Nobody slept with Mommy while you were gone!"

☛ A farm wife was entertaining the small son of a friend. "Are you sure, Mikey," she said, "that you can cut your own meat?"

"I think so," Mikey replied. "We've had it this tough at home before, too."

☛ The small daughter remarked on the large size of her mother's tummy. "Yes, darling," Mommy replied. "You see, Daddy has given me a little baby."

Astonished, the little girl rushed into the next room. "Daddy," she cried, "did you give Mommy a little baby?"

"Well, yes, I did," her father said.

"Well," exclaimed the daughter, "She's eaten it!"

☛ A fat lady got on a scale outside the dime store and the hand spun all the way around. The little girl watching in amazement, gasped and said, "Don't tell me you get all that for a penny."

☛ "Are we going to take our cat with us when you and I go to visit Grandma next week?" five-year-old Penelope asked.

"Why no, dear, of course not," replied her mother. "Whatever made you think so?"

"Well," Penelope said, "I heard Daddy tell Mr. Smith from across the road that the 'mouse' would have a fine time when the 'cat' was away next week."

Teenagers

"Cute teenagers exist only on television, I suspect. I know there are none in my neighborhood."

—Robert MacKenzie

Chapter 29

The Wonder Years

"The best way to keep teenagers at home is to make the home atmosphere pleasant—and let the air out of the tires."
—*Dorothy Parker*

☞ Weary of the constant disorder in her son's room, a mother laid down the law. "For every item I have to pick up off the floor," she declared, "You will have to pay me a dime."

At the end of the week, her son owed her $1.70. She received the money promptly, along with a 50-cent tip and a note that read, "Thanks, Mom, keep up the good work!"

☞ In this modern era during the new "mop-top" haircut rage, a disturbed father said, "Son, go get your hair cut—it looks like a mop."

His son replied, "Dad, what's a mop?"

☞ The teenager told his father, "Dad, instead of buying me an expensive birthday present this year, why not give me something you've made yourself."

The skeptical father responded, "Like what?"

"Money!"

☞ Children grow up so quickly. One day you look at your car's gas gauge showing empty and then you realize they're teenagers.

☞ "Mind if I use the car tonight, Lenny?" the farmer dryly asked his teenage son.

"Why?" his son asked.

"Well," said the father, "I'm taking your mother out and I want to impress her."

☛ "My son," complained the irate farmer, "is a lazy, good-for-nothing fellow. He won't work, he won't help around the house and he won't get up until the first rays of sunlight hit his window."

"Isn't that rather early for him to get up?" asked the farmer's neighbor.

"No, you don't understand," he said. "His room faces west."

☛ Two teenage farm boys were talking at the hamburger stand in town. One said, "I had a long talk with my father about girls. He doesn't know anything about them either."

☛ A policeman approached a man sitting on the sidewalk at three in the morning. "What are you doing out here so late?" the cop asked.

The man replied, "I lost the key to my house and I'm waiting for one of the kids to come home and let me in."

☛ As the party-bound teenage daughter flew out the door, her father yelled to her, "Don't rush home, Jennifer. I have a lot of calls to catch up on."

☛ Two wheat farmers who hadn't seen each other since their school days ran into each other at the state fair. After they chatted for a while, one of the farmers said his teenage son was so silly he thought he was studying to be a lunatic.

The other farmer nodded and said his son was a raving idiot, and a great argument ensued as to whose son was the sillier.

Finally, one of the men called his boy over and said, "Ralph, here are two dollars. I want you to go into the city and buy your mother a deep freezer."

Then the other farmer called his son, and gave him two dollars as well. "Warren, my boy," he said, "I'd like you to go to my hotel in the city—you know where it is—and find out if I'm there."

The two lads met on the bus. Ralph said, "My old man's crazy. He gave me two bucks to get Mom a deep freezer, but he didn't say whether to get an upright or chest model."

"He's not as loony as mine," Warren said. "He gave me two dollars and told me to go to his hotel in the city and see if he was there. What a nut! He could have called himself and found out for a quarter."

☛ Age 15 is when a boy takes up weightlifting but can't pick up his socks.

☛ Two teenage hippies went to an art gallery and one of them stared at a display and griped, "I hate this modern art garbage."

The other said, "Get with it, man, that's a mirror."

☛ *Teenager*: An appetite wearing $89 sneakers.

☛ As her two teenage sons walked across the barnyard together toward the garage, the mother leaned out the window and called, "You boys will have to double up with the convertible tonight. Your father broke the chain on his bicycle and has to go to town."

☛ A man took his teenage daughter on a trip to New York City. They went to a Broadway play that made the father blush a bit.

"I'm sorry, Dorothy, that I brought you here," he said. "This is hardly a place for a girl of your age."

"Oh, that's all right, Dad," Dorothy said. "It'll probably liven up a bit before too long."

☛ The old man was in the hospital recovering from a serious operation. It was his birthday and he had received no cards or presents from his family.

But the next day, three of his teenage sons came to visit, all empty-handed. After some brief conversation, the old man could stand it no longer and said, "Well, I see you all forgot it was poor old Dad's birthday."

The sons were embarrassed and explained they had all been busy and just forgot.

"That's OK," said the old man. "I guess I can forgive you. Forgetfulness runs in our family. I even forgot to marry your mother."

"Good heavens!" exclaimed the boys. "Why that means we're..."

"That's right," replied their father. "And darn cheap ones at that!"

☛ You know your kids are teenagers when they quit asking where they came from and start refusing to tell you where they're going.

☞ A farmer was telling the hired hand how worried he was about his son. "What's wrong with him?" the hired man asked. The farmer replied, "The kid is weird."

"How so?"

"Well, for instance," the farmer explained, "this morning he Scotch-taped all the worms to the sidewalk and then watched the birds get hernias."

☞ Two cannibals opened a restaurant. The menu read: "Men—$1.50; Women—$2.50; Teenagers—$25.00."

A customer went in and asked why they charged so much more to order a teenager.

The cannibal replied, "Did you ever try to clean one of those devils?"

☞ Steve and his dad got into one of their verbal wars again at the dinner table. "When George Washington was your age," the father told his son, "he was already a surveyor and earning good money."

"So what?" Steve replied sharply. "When he was your age, he was president of the United States."

☞ A farmer called up the telephone company and ordered a 50-foot extension cord put on the phone. He explained, "I want my daughter to stay outside now that the weather is nice."

☞ Two teenagers on a tour of a modern art gallery found themselves alone in a room of modern sculpture. Staring at the twisted pipes, broken glass and tangled shapes, one of them said, "Hey, let's get out of here before they accuse us of wrecking this place."

☞ Some farm families can trace their ancestors back for hundreds of years but can't tell you where their children were last night.

☞ The farmer approached his teenage son. "What happened to that water-proof, shock-proof, unbreakable, anti-magnetic watch I gave you?" he asked.

"I lost it," came the reply.

☛ "So, your son drives a car now," a neighbor said to a farmer. "How long did it take him to learn?"

"About 2 1/2 cars," replied the farmer sadly.

☛ "I'm looking for adventure, excitement and beautiful women," the young teenager proclaimed to his dad as he prepared to leave the farm. "Don't try to stop me!"

"Who's trying to stop you?" shouted the father. "I'm going with you!"

☛ "My teenage daughter gave us a bad time last night," a farmer told a farm worker. "She started to run away from home. Luckily, she never got past the front door."

"What happened?" asked the worker.

The farmer exclaimed, "The telephone rang."

☛ A conscientious mother, keenly alert to current drug problems among today's youth, was horrified by a note she found in her son's pocket.

"Can you explain this, Freddie?" she said, confronting him. "Puff, puff, drag, puff, puff, puff?"

"Sure," the boy replied, "I'm learning the Star Spangled Banner on my harmonica."

☛ "Hi-ho, Mommy-O," said the teenage daughter, trying to appear very cool. "Can I hit the flicks tonight?"

"What are you talking about?" asked the puzzled mother. "What do you mean 'hit the flicks?' What kind of talk is that?"

"That's just 'teen talk' for going to the movies," the girl explained disdainfully.

"Well, all right, dear," said the mother dubiously. "You may hit the flicks after you spread the bed, scour the shower and swish the dishes."

☛ Teenagers are people who hear the word "loafers" and think of shoes. Parents are people who hear the word "loafers" and think of teenagers.

☛ "Now that your daughter has a license, does she want to drive your car all the time?" the farm equipment dealer asked his customer.

"No, not all the time," the customer said. "She always turns the car over to me when the gas tank needs refilling."

☛ A classified ad seen in a rural newspaper: "For sale, complete set of World Book Encyclopedia. Never used—teenager daughter already knew everything."

☛ Two senior citizens were sitting on a park bench. "You know what, Clem?" the first one said. "I survived World War II, four auto accidents, two bad marriages, two depressions, 13 company strikes, three mortgages and all the government farm policies—and now some wise teenager tells me I don't know what life is all about!"

☛ The farmer's teenage daughter had been on the phone for half an hour. When she finally hung up, her father yelled from the kitchen, "You usually talk for two hours. What stopped you?"

His daughter replied, "Wrong number."

☛ A farm mother walked into kitchen and saw the all-too-familiar sight of her son kneeling in front of the fridge. "For once I'd like to come into the kitchen and not see you rummaging through the refrigerator," she said.

He replied wisely, "Then try whistling as you come down the hall."

☛ A rancher was buying a watch for his son's birthday gift. "I suppose," said the clerk, "that it's going to be a surprise."

"I'll say," the father. "He's expecting a convertible."

☛ Two mothers were comparing notes on their teenage sons. One was saying, "I have to drag Bobby out of bed every morning to get him to school on time."

"Oh, I never have any problems with Tommy. I just toss our cat into bed with him and he gets up right away," the second mother informed her.

"How does that work?"

"Well, it's pretty simple," she said. "Tommy sleeps with the dog."

☛ A farmer was telling his neighbor about his teenage son who was kicked out of the zoo for feeding the monkeys.

"What?" the neighbor asked. "For feeding the monkeys?"

"Yeah," the farmer replied. "They found out he was feeding them to the lions."

☛ Two rural parents, each a chaperone at a high school party, were chewing the fat when suddenly one woman exclaimed, "Just look at that youngster, the one with the long straight hair, a cigarette and tight trousers. Is it a boy or a girl?"

"It's a boy—my son," was the reply.

"Please forgive me, ma'am, I never would have been so outspoken if I had known you were his mother," she said apologetically.

"I'm not. I'm his father."

Chapter 30

Students Of Life

"The best way to see America nowadays is to try to get your son, or daughter, into college."

—*Earl Wilson*

High School Days

"A father who wants his children to get an education these days might have to pull a few wires—the television wire, the hi-fi wire and the radio wire."

—*Lavonne Mathison*

☛ A son brought his report card in to his father. "Dad," he said, "here's my report card and here's one of yours I found in the attic."

☛ A high school freshman just couldn't seem to behave. Nearly every day he was sent to the principal's office for one thing or another.

The principal said, "This is the fifth time that you have been sent to my office this week for misbehaving. Now what do you have to say for yourself?"

"I'm glad it's Friday," he said.

☛ The teacher said, "Today's lesson teaches us about the influence of kings and queens. But there is a higher power. Who can tell me what it is?"

Vinnie piped up, "Aces."

☛ It was a bright spring morning and four high school boys decided to skip classes. Arriving at school after lunch, they explained to the teacher that their car had a flat tire along the way.

To their relief, the teacher smiled understandingly and said, "You boys missed a test this morning. Please take seats apart from one another and get out your paper and pencil."

When the boys were seated, she continued, "Answer this question, 'Which tire was flat?'"

☛ A mountaineer took his son down to the high school to enroll him. "My boy's after larnin', what d'ya have?" he asked the teacher.

"We offer English, trigonometry, Spanish, etc.," she replied.

"Well, give him some of that trigonometry," he said. "He's the worst shot in the family."

☛ "Randy," the teacher said, "what are the three great American parties?"

Randy said, "Democratic, Republican and cocktail."

☛ A farmer had a visitor who asked, "What is your son going to be when he gets out of high school?"

The farmer replied, "Looks now like he'll be an old man."

☛ A farmer was telling his hired hand how he finally cured his 17-year-old son of habitually being late to school. "I bought him a car," he said.

"But how did that help?"

"Well," replied the father, "he has to get going an hour earlier to find a place in the school parking lot."

☛ "Who can give me a definition of false economy?" the teacher asked.

A farm girl in the front answered, "A man who takes such long steps to save his $10-shoes that he splits his $20-trousers."

☛ After reading his son's high school report card, a farmer said to his son, "I'm worried about you being at the bottom of your class."

"Don't worry about it, Dad," his son assured him. "They teach the same thing at both ends."

☛ The high school English teacher said, "An abstract noun is something you can think of, but you can't touch it. Can you give me an example of one?"

Pete said, "Sure. My father's new car."

College Life

"I have a son in college, and when he's home there's no food in the refrigerator. And I can't get food for the refrigerator because there's no gas in the car.

"And I can't put gas in the car because there's no money in the sugar bowl. And I can't put money in the sugar bowl because I have a son in college."

☛ Smith and Jones were discussing their families. "How is your son, Jim, doing at the agricultural college?" Smith asked.

"OK," replied Jones, "he recently completed a course in journalism."

"You don't say. Does he write for money?"

"Yes, indeed," Jones said. "I hear from him at least once a week."

☛ One nice thing about having a son in college is the letters you get. Like the one that reads: "Dear Dad, Haven't heard from you. Hope you haven't been ill. Send me a check so I'll know you're all right."

☞ A college freshman was complaining to his roommate in the dorm. "I'll never trust my parents again," he said. "I asked them for $600 for an encyclopedia and they sent me the encyclopedia."

☞ Two farmers were talking about college and its escalating tuition costs. "Has your son's college education proved of any real value?" one asked.

"Yes, indeed," the other farmer said. "It's entirely cured his mother of bragging about him."

☞ The freshman's father paid his farm son a surprise visit. Arriving at 1 a.m., he banged on the fraternity house door. A voice from the second floor yelled, "Whaddya want?"

"Does Harvey Chapman live here?" asked the father.

"Yeah," answered the voice, "just drag him in."

☞ Pity the student who has to decide whether to graduate at mid-year and face a cold, cruel world or wait until June when it's just as cruel but not as cold.

☞ Three college students were visiting a foreign country. One was from the University of Wisconsin, another from Michigan State University and the third was an ag engineering student from Purdue University.

Anyway, they were in a country with a tyrannical ruler and extremely cruel laws. And, for not removing their shoes when walking past the dictator's portrait, they were sentenced to death by guillotine.

This was pretty harsh, but the executioner told them they didn't have much to worry about. The guillotine hadn't worked in years. What's more, when it failed to whack off their heads, they could go free.

The Wisconsin student was first. The executioner pulled the rope and the blade didn't fall. He was set free. The same thing happened to the Michigan State student.

Then the ag engineering student from Purdue was led to the guillotine. Before he was strapped in, he looked at the rope pull and latch, then turned to the executioner.

"You know, I think I've already figured out what's wrong with this thing..."

☞ A student in a college health class raised his hand and asked, "It says here that if you study hard, don't drink or smoke or run around with girls, you'll live longer. Is that true?"

"We don't know for sure," the professor answered. "Nobody's ever tried it."

☛ The young man had just returned from the agricultural college for the summer and was showing off to a neighboring farmer.

"Your methods are so old-fashioned," the student declared. "Why, I'll bet you don't get 10 pounds of apples from that tree."

"I dare say you're right," the farmer said. "That's a pear tree."

☛ The college professor stood at the podium and said, "I will not begin today's lecture until the room settles down."

A freshman country boy yelled from the back, "Why don't you go home and sleep it off?"

☛ A farmer was overheard saying at the bar, "My son is majoring in both economics and applied physics in college. It's not a very useful combination, but it does explain how he can spend money at the speed of light."

☛ An agricultural student had been pestering his father for a new car. On a visit to campus, the parent pointed out that most of the cars in the parking lot were quite old.

"But Dad," the youth protested, "those cars belong to the faculty!"

☛ At the local agricultural college, a senior received a grant to study crickets. After collecting the insects in a mason jar, he soon had enough to begin the experiments.

Setting a cricket on the lab table, the student said, "Jump! Jump! Jump!" The cricket jumped six times, and he recorded it in his notebook.

Then the student pulled off one of the cricket's legs. He yelled, "Jump! Jump! Jump!" but this time it only jumped four times, and he wrote it into his notes.

The student then removed the cricket's other leg and once again ordered the cricket to jump. It didn't move. He raised his voice, but the cricket still didn't jump. "I said 'jump,' you stupid cricket!" he yelled again. But still, there was no movement.

The student thought about it, then wrote in his notebook, "Cricket went deaf."

☞ The instructor in atomic warfare asked his class, "What's the difference between radiation and contamination?"

A freshman, fresh off the farm, thought for a moment and came up with an answer. "Radiation," he drawled, "is when you smell manure. Contamination is when you step in it."

☞ The mountain youth returned from college on semester break. "What are ye larnin', son?" his pa inquired.

"Well, Pa, I'm studying algebra."

"That's fine, son," the old man said. "Say something in algebra."

Not wishing to let his father down, the youth proclaimed solemnly, "Pie-R Squared."

The old man exploded. "If that's what they're larnin' ye, ye can stop school right now! Everybody knows pie are round! Cornbread are square!"

☞ Sending a child through college these days is very educational. It teaches parents how to do without a lot of things.

Hangin' Up The Boots

"By the time a man finds greener pastures, he's too old to climb the fence."

Chapter 31

Wrinkles, Aches And Pains

"Life is just a symphony of snap, crackle and pop. When you're young, it's cereal. When you're older, it's your joints."

☛ An elderly farm couple was having trouble remembering things. While they were watching the afternoon game shows on TV, the farmer said to his wife, "Honey, how would you like me to get you a little ice cream?"

"That sounds wonderful," the wife answered. "But I think you should write it down so you don't forget it."

"No, I won't forget a little ice cream," the farmer said. "How would you like a little chocolate on it?"

"I'd love a little chocolate sauce on my ice cream," his wife added. "Now write those down, so you make sure you don't forget."

Again, the husband refused to write it down, assuring her he wouldn't forget, and he left for the kitchen.

A few moments later, he returned into the room carrying two plates of scrambled eggs.

"I told you to write it down," his wife exclaimed. "You forgot the toast!"

☛ The oldest man in the small farm town was addressing the local Boy Scout troop. After a long speech about honesty and decency, he said, "Boys, let me tell you this. I have never taken a drink. I have never smoked a cigarette. I have never gone to bed after 10 p.m. I have never left the table over-full. I have never looked at another woman but my wife. Tomorrow I'll celebrate my 87th birthday."

There was a pause, then a voice from the back asked, "How?"

☞ At their 50th wedding anniversary party, Gus turned to his bride of 50 years and said, "I'm proud of you."

The wife complained, "What did you say? You know I can't hear what you are saying without my hearing aid."

"I'm proud of you," the man shouted.

"That's all right," she nodded. "I'm tired of you, too."

☞ A 75-year-old man was a streaker. One day he ran up to a young woman and asked her, "How do you like my birthday suit?"

She checked him over and answered, "Looks like it needs ironing."

☞ An elderly farmer decided to get a physical examination before finally retiring. After all the tests, the doctor told him he was fine, especially for a man of his age.

"You must come from good lineage to have the body of a man 30 years younger than you are," the doctor said. "How old was your father when he died?"

"Who said he died?" the farmer said. "He's over 80, walks three miles a day, holds a full-time job and still chops the firewood himself."

"That's wonderful," the doctor said, amazed. "How old was your grandfather when he passed away?"

"But he didn't pass away. He's alive and kicking at 101 and in two weeks he's getting married."

The doctor shook his head and asked, "What man in his right mind would want to get married at his age?"

The farmer replied, "Did I say he wanted to get married?"

☞ Five-year-old Billy asked his grandfather, "Are you still growing?"

"Why do you ask, child?" inquired the grandfather.

Billy explained, "Well, the top of your head's coming through the hair!"

☞ Two grade-schoolers were discussing old age when one of the kids said, "I wonder if old people have any fun."

The other turned and said, "Well, seems like every time you hear about a 100-year-old, he's having a party."

☞ An old farm wife was having her portrait painted for her children and asked the artist if he would paint jeweled rings on her fingers, pearls on her neck, diamond earrings in her ears, and jeweled bracelets on both wrists.

"Sure," said the artist, "but may I ask why?"

"Because I don't have long to live," the old lady explained. "I know that my husband has a young girlfriend. When I die, I want to drive her crazy trying to find out what happened to my jewelry."

☛ Old Lenny was bragging about his new hearing aid. "It's the most expensive one I've ever had," he said. "It cost $2,500."

Someone asked, "What kind is it?"

Lenny shouted, "Half-past four."

☛ Little Suzie returned from Sunday School and ran into the lap of her grandfather and asked, "Were you on the Ark, Grandpa, when the flood came?"

"No, certainly not," replied the old man.

Puzzled, the little girl asked, "Well, then why weren't you drowned?"

☛ At a family reunion, an 87-year-old retired cattle rancher was the life of the party. Someone asked him to describe his daily routine.

"Well," he said, "first, I have the morning paper brought to me in bed. Then I turn to the obituary section and if my name isn't there, I get up."

☛ On the beach in Florida, a retired farmer watched a group of shapely young girls in bikinis doing their morning exercises.

"Do you think this sort of thing is really good for reducing?" his sour-faced friend said.

"Certainly," the old farmer replied. "I walk three miles every day just to watch it."

☛ "Doctor," old Charlie said, "I'm suffering from a pain in my right leg."

"Well, there's no cure," the doctor said. "It's just old age."

"You must be mistaken, Doc. The left leg is as old as the right and it doesn't hurt me at all."

☛ Old Henry, in his mid-80s, is as unconscious of his age as a 20-year-old. One cold day, he walked into the house all wet and muddy from his knees down. "What happened?" his wife asked.

"I wanted to cross the creek to see about the cow," he explained. "I used to jump it clear and easy, but now every dang time I try it, I land in the middle. Guess I just ain't noticed it getting wider."

☞ A reporter was interviewing the old codger who was celebrating his 100th birthday. "What accomplishment are you most proud of?" he asked.

"Well," said the man, "I've lived 100 years and haven't a single enemy in the world."

"What a beautiful thought," commented the writer. "How truly inspirational."

"Yep," the man added, "outlived every last one of them!"

☞ The stingy old farmer, who was almost deaf, decided that buying a hearing aid was too expensive. Instead, he told his neighbor, he just wrapped an ordinary piece of wire around his ear.

"How can that help you hear better?" his neighbor shouted.

"Now," he said, "everybody talks louder."

☞ Up in the Smoky Mountains, it's rumored that people take it easy and therefore live longer. John, the postman in town, was on his route when he stumbled across one of his uncles—82 years old. The man was sitting on a stump crying his eyes out.

"What's wrong?" John asked.

"Pa whipped me," his old uncle said, sobbing.

"What for?"

Between tears, the old man said, "For throwing rocks at Grandpa."

☞ An elderly couple was sitting on the porch when a serious conversation arose again. "You know, Pa, we're getting along in our years, and I suppose one of us will be passing along soon."

Her husband answered, "Oh now, Ma, don't you start takin' on about that."

"I ain't, Pa," she replied. "But I've been thinking when it happens, I'd like to move to Florida."

☞ During one of the most intense moments of a murder movie, an old man groped for something on the movie house

169

floor. He was greatly disturbing the lady in the next seat, who finally turned and asked testily, "What did you lose?"

"A caramel," said the man.

She barked, "You're going to all this bother for a measly caramel?"

"Yes," was the reply. "My teeth are in it."

☛ Two couples in their 80s were sitting around wondering what to do for the evening, when one old-timer whispered to his friend, "Hey, Leo, let's all go to a motel."

So, they all piled into the car and drove to the closest motel. While checking in, Leo said, "Hey, Joe, whaddaya say we swap partners tonight?" Joe agreed and they did.

An hour or so later, Leo turned to Joe and said, "This is fun...but I wonder what the two girls are doing in their room?"

☛ Two boys who did demolition work in the Navy returned home to the farm. They were dying to show their dad how they could remove one of the old shacks on the farm with dynamite.

After constant pestering, the father finally said, "OK, you can blast the old outhouse behind the garage."

The two boys spent six days getting the dynamite set just right. When they were ready to set it off, they called everybody out of the house to watch. They had their father do the honors, and as he pushed on the lever, the outhouse rocketed high in the air and landed right back down on the foundation.

To everyone's surprise, the outhouse door opened and out came Grandpa. He staggered out, muttering, "Boys, don't ever eat any of Grandma's beans."

☛ "I don't plan to get married until I find a girl just like the girl who married my grandfather," the farm hand stated at the local tavern.

One of the guys said, "Man, they don't make women like that anymore."

"Oh, I don't know," he said. "Grandpa married this one just last week!"

☛ On the porch of a general store in a small crossroads town, two old-timers were talking about the good old days when one of them said that a good sound "licking" was necessary for kids to learn and remember. But his blowhard friend disagreed and was about to disclose one his stories. "The only time I was ever licked," he said, "was for telling the truth."

There was silence for a moment and then his friend quietly said, "Well, Sam, it sure cured you."

☛ Two retired farmers were playing checkers in the barber shop and discussing how badly their wives were aging. "You know, Jake, my wife's arms must be getting shorter. When we got married, she could reach all the way around me."

☛ An old spinster claimed her eyesight was fine regardless of what all the other ladies thought. To prove her point, she stuck a pin in a tree and the next day while walking with one of her friends, she said, "Isn't that a pin sticking in that tree?"

Her friend was shocked. But as the spinster went to retrieve the pin from the tree, she tripped over a cow.

☛ "I got so cold last night I couldn't sleep," Grandpa said. "I just shivered."

"Did your teeth chatter?" little Katie asked.

"I don't know," he said. "We don't sleep together."

☛ Two retired farmers were standing on Main Street discussing the affairs of the day. Neither could hear too well. One turned and asked his friend, "What do you think about LSD?"

The other farmer cleared his throat and said sharply, "The best president we ever had."

☛ A bitter old country lady was bitten by a mad dog and was advised to prepare her will because there was the possibility of rabies. She wrote furiously for two hours.

"It looks like an unusually long will," her lawyer said.

"Will? Who's writing a will?" the old witch snapped. "That's a list of the people I'm going to bite."

☛ The retired farmer stopped to chat with a fellow old-timer on the street one afternoon. As they were parting, the man asked, "Which way was I going when we stopped to talk?"

Pointing, his friend answered, "That way."

"Oh good," he said as he headed off down the street. "That means I've had my lunch."

☛ The teacher asked, "Can any of my bright students tell me why a man's hair turns gray quicker than his mustache?"

After a moment, one hand went up. "Sure, teach," said the boy. "It's because his hair had a 20-year head-start on his mustache."

☛ The elderly woman who lived alone in the quaint stone house on the top of the hill was thought by the neighbors to be a bit eccentric.

One old man was quite sure something was wrong when he paused in the road and saw the strange old woman holding a sprinkling can above a flower box.

He called out, "Ma'am, there's no bottom in that sprinkling can."

"It's quite all right," she answered. "These are artificial flowers I'm watering."

☛ A cranky old man invested in one of those new hearing aids that are almost invisible. A few days later he returned to the store to express his delight.

"I'll bet your family likes it too," the salesman said.

"Oh, they don't know I've got it," the old man said. "And am I having a ball! In the past two days, I've changed my will twice."

☛ "A man is never older than he feels," said the philosophical farmer. "Now, this morning I feel like a two-year-old!"

To which his wife said, "A horse or egg?"

☛ Old Dwight, who was 89, was about to marry a 23-year-old girl. He was so excited that he bought a huge house next to the school yard. But, the girl was no fool and she said, "We're going to go down and have a physical examination."

The 23-year-old girl had her physical first and then Dwight was given his examination. Shortly afterward, the doctor called the couple in and said, "I don't like to tell you this, but the consummation of your marriage could be fatal."

There was dead silence for a few moments and then Dwight piped up, "Well, if she dies, she dies!"

☛ After celebrating their 50th wedding anniversary, Clem and Sarah were lying in bed reflecting on the day's happenings and their long and successful marriage.

"Do you remember, dear, when you used to be so romantic

and nip at my ears?" Sarah asked.
"Sure do, honey," Clem said.
"Please do it again," Sarah said.
"OK," Clem said, hopping out of bed.
"Where are you going?"
Clem replied, "To get my teeth."

☛ Three old codgers at the old folks' home were discussing the way they wanted to die. The first said he'd like to be driving an Indy race car and drive it into the wall on one of those turns.

The second recalled his first plane ride and said he'd like his end to come in a jet plane flying faster than the speed of sound.

The third, who just turned 95, thought for a bit before offering his opinion. "Well, if it was up to me," he said, "I'd like to be shot in bed by that young nurse's jealous husband."

☛ Young Penelope had been visiting with an elderly neighbor man. When she got home, she breathlessly told her mother about the man. "He must be the richest man in the world," she said. "He has gold in his teeth, silver in his hair, stones in the kidneys and gas in his stomach!"

☛ An elderly gentleman tugged at a high school boy's sleeve during a fashion show and said, "Here I am at 75, and when I look at these models, I wish I was 20 years older."

The kid was thrown off and asked, "You mean 20 years younger, don't you?"

"No, I mean 20 years older," the senior citizen said. "Then I wouldn't give a darn about them."

Chapter 32

Wise Men Say...

*"Age is a question of mind over matter.
If you don't mind, it doesn't matter."*

—Satchel Paige

☞ Nothing makes you feel older than the discovery that today's school children are studying in history class what you studied in current events.

☞ Grandpa says you'll always stay young if you live honestly, eat slowly, sleep sufficiently, work industriously, worship faithfully—and lie about your age.

☞ Two elderly farm women were talking as their husbands were glued to a steamy movie on cable TV. The first woman asked, "What goes 10, 9, 8, 7, 6, 5, 4, 3, 2, 1?"
The other woman shrugged her shoulders.
The first one said, "Bo Derek growing old."

☞ Grandpa says, "I'm getting a new TV set. I've seen everything at least twice on my old one."

☞ It's another sign of old age when you begin to spend more time talking with your druggist than with your bartender.

☞ Grandpa says he reads *Playboy* for the same reason he reads *National Geographic*—to look at sights he's never gonna visit.

☞ An old-timer is a person whose annual property tax exceeds what he paid for the darn place in the beginning.

☞ Grandpa says that even back in his day there was something to make you sleep. They called it work!

☞ You know you're getting old when the little gray-haired lady you help across the street is your wife.

☞ Grandpa observes, "When you reach a certain age, everything seems to wear out, spread out or fall out."

☞ By the time you're rich enough to sleep late, you're so old you always wake up early.

☞ Grandpa says he doesn't worry about his gray hair. "Gray hair is great—ask any bald guy."

☞ When married couples are young, they sit close together because they're in love. When they're old, they sit close together so they can hear each other.

☞ Grandpa claims there are three stages in a man's life: Youth, middle age and "you never looked better."

☞ An old-timer is one who remembers when "seatbelts" were a juvenile corrective measure—not a safety device.

☞ Grandpa says fun is like insurance—the older you get, the more it costs.

☞ Old age is the time of your life when you don't care where your wife goes, just as long as you don't have to go with her.

☞ Grandpa says he has reached the "cereal" age. He's beginning to feel his corns more than his oats.

☞ Old age does have some benefits. For instance, you can whistle as you wash your teeth.

☞ An old-timer is one who can remember when a babysitter was called mother.

☛ Grandpa likes to recall the "Good Ol' Days," when a family had one car, one radio, one telephone, one bank account—and one mortgage.

☛ Grandpa remembers the Depression this way: "People in the big towns used to go downtown on Saturday nights and watch haircuts. The best we could do was to go down to the lumberyard and watch wood warp."

☛ Old age is when the scales tell you that you weigh twice as much as when you were 20 and your wife tells you that you know only half as much.

☛ Grandpa remarks that Mother Nature is generous. When we reach the sitting-around stage of life, she provides us with more cushion.

☛ Grandpa observes, "At my age, by the time I find temptation, I'm too tired to give in to it."

☛ Grandpa has this advice: "Before deciding to retire in town, stay in the house for a week and watch the daytime TV shows.

☛ Grandpa observes, "You're an old-timer if you can remember when air and water were clean and sex was dirty."

☛ Grandpa warns that old age is a period of life when you'll do almost anything to feel better except give up what's hurting you.

☛ You know you're getting old when you feel like the morning after when you haven't been anywhere the night before.

☛ Grandpa observes: "Youth is that part of life when you are always looking for greener fields. When you reach old age, you can't even mow the one you've got."

Three-Piece Suits

*"I resent large corporations.
They flatten personalities."*

—*Bob Newhart*

Chapter 33

Our Smiling Bankers

"A banker is a man who lends you an umbrella when the weather is fair and takes it away from you when it rains."

☛ A farmer with his friendly dog entered the bank and applied for a loan so he could buy more land.

The banker obtained the necessary information, but then turned down the loan. As he told the farmer the bad news, the dog bit the banker, cornered a customer in the bank and bit him, too.

The banker said to the farmer, "I can understand why your dog bit me, but why in the world did he have to bite that poor customer?"

The farmer replied, "To get the rotten taste out of his mouth."

☛ The farmer fidgeted in the chair while his rural banker reviewed his latest loan application. "Your assets seem to be in order," said the banker. "But tell me about your liabilities."

"No problem," the farmer said. "I can lie with the best of them."

☛ We've now reached the Seven Dwarfs stage of taking out a mortgage. When you go into the bank, you're Bashful. When you hear mortgages are still available, you're Happy. When you're told the rate, you're Grumpy. And if you accept it, you're Dopey.

☛ Two farmers were talking at the mill. "Say, Dusty," one said, "how's your banker treating you?"

"He's helping me get back on my feet," Dusty answered. "Just yesterday he repossessed my pickup truck."

☞ The holdup man shoved a note at the bank teller, ordering: "Hand me all the dough in your cage. I've got you covered."

The teller scribbled her reply: "Kindly go to the next window; I'm on my lunch hour."

☞ Grandpa observes that if you want to write something that will last forever, sign a mortgage.

☞ The banker wrote a collection letter to Ernie, a farmer who was constantly late in payments. The banker's letter began: "Dear Ernie, we are surprised that we have not received anything from you..."

A few days later, the letter came back with a hand-written scrawl across the bottom of the page. Ernie wrote: "There's no reason to be surprised. I didn't send anything."

☞ The feed mill credit manager asked a customer, "Do you have much money in the bank?"

"I don't know," replied the farmer. "I haven't shaken it lately."

☞ The gunman rushed into a bank and said, "Give me all the money you've got!"

The bank teller said, "Here, take the books, too. I'm $10,000 short."

☞ Attacked by two thieves, a farmer put up a terrific fight. Finally, the two thugs overcame him and searched his pockets. When they found only a dime, they were amazed.

"Why would you put up such a fight and risk getting killed just for a dime?" one of the outlaws asked.

"Well," replied the farmer, "the truth of the matter is, I didn't want my financial condition to be exposed."

☞ Many financial institutions today use high-technology surveillance cameras to reduce the possibility of thefts. However, there's a big difference in how banks and savings and loans utilize this system.

In banks, the cameras are positioned in the lobbies to eliminate the possibility of bank robberies by those entering the bank. But in savings and loan institutions, you'll find cameras aren't pointed at customers. They're all in the executive offices watching the president and vice president.

☛ The syndicated newspaper advice column, "Ask Ann Marie," recently received a letter from a farmer, who wrote: "Dear Ann Marie, I have two brothers. One is a banker. The other was sent to the electric chair. My mother died in an insane asylum. Since I was three years old, my father has been a narcotics pusher. One of my sisters is a successful and highly-respected prostitute, while the other is the common-law wife of the leader of the Hell's Angels.

"Recently, I met a wonderful girl shortly after she was released from prison for smothering her illegitimate baby. We are very, very much in love and expect to be married just as soon as her communicable disease clears up.

"My question is this—should I tell her about my brother, the banker?"

☛ The district supervisor of the First National Bank decided to do a spot check one Friday afternoon at one of his branches.

When he arrived, he found the doors had been closed a half an hour early. Using his master key, he tiptoed in and saw that six staff members, including the manager, were in the back room playing poker.

He thought, "I'll give these boys and girls one heck of a shock." He pressed the bank's alarm button. Then he waited.

In five minutes, the bartender from across the street came over with a six-pack of beer.

☛ A banker met with one of his farm clients. "Now that you've paid off the loan, we're glad to give you the deed," the banker said.

The farmer answered, "Well, if you don't mind, just give me a mortgage."

"Don't you know the difference between a deed and a mortgage?"

"Not really," said the farmer. "All I know is I had a farm during the Depression. I had a deed and the bank had a mortgage, and they ended up with the farm."

☛ A farmer had to have a heart transplant and was told by the doctors to choose the organ from one of three donors—a 17-year-old high school student, a track star or a banker.

He took the heart of the banker—figuring it had never been used.

☞ The deceased farm credit officer appeared at the gates of Hell and asked to get in.

"Why did you come here?" Satan demanded.

"I want to collect some old accounts from a couple of my former customers who have died before me."

"How do you know they are here?" Satan asked.

"Well," he said, "every time I tried to collect, this is the place they recommended."

☞ The farm equipment salesman, about to start his own dealership, strode into the bank and asked to borrow $50,000.

"We'll see," said the bank president. "Can you give me a statement?"

"Yes," the man said. "And you can quote me. I'm very optimistic."

☞ Duke wanted to join a notorious gang. The head of the gang said, "It's not easy to get into this mob. What's your record?"

"Well," Duke said, "I robbed the First National Bank and the Third National Bank."

"What's the matter with the Second National Bank?" the gang leader asked.

Duke replied, "Nothing. That's where I keep my money."

☞ After selling his beef herd at a loss, the cattle raiser poured out a tale of woe to his banker. "I've got some bad news and some good news," he told the loan arranger. "The bad news is that I marketed my beef at a loss and I can't pay the overdue notes you are holding."

The banker, shaking his head, asked, "So what's the good news?"

The farmer added, "The good news is that I'm going to keep on banking with you."

☞ Two bankers were talking over lunch. One said, "You know, James, I finally got that farmer, Johnson, to pay his debts."

"Really?" the other asked. "How did you do it?"

He explained, "I sent him a letter that said if he didn't pay his bill to us by the first of the month, I was going to tell the rest of his creditors he did."

☞ Three men died and went to Heaven on the same day. The first was the Pope, the second was Billy Graham and the third was a banker.

As St. Peter led them down the golden streets to usher them to their eternal homes, he stopped in front of three buildings—two tiny shacks and one immense mansion. St. Peter directed the Pope and the Reverend Graham to the shacks. Then he rolled out the red carpet and told the banker to move his things into the mansion.

Both Billy Graham and the Pope quietly inquired why two great servants like themselves would spend eternity in cozy, but unattractive shacks while a banker was spending eternity in a mansion.

St. Peter replied, "Hey guys, we've got lots of preachers and popes up here in Heaven. But this is our first banker!"

☞ A banker was proud of his meticulous glass eye. Imported from France, it looked so real that no one ever questioned whether it was real or not.

But one day a farmer who had been turned down for a loan said, "How'd you lose your eye?"

The banker was shocked and said, "I can't believe it! How did you know I had a glass eye?"

The farmer replied, "I picked out the glass eye because that one had a little glimmer of warmth in it."

☞ What's the difference between a dead skunk and a dead banker on a rural highway?

There are skid marks in front of the skunk.

☞ It seems ridiculous to spend millions of dollars developing nuclear bombs. We already have something that destroys people and leaves buildings standing. It's called a 14% mortgage.

☞ Old bankers never die—they just lose interest.

☞ A stranger in town asked a shoeshine boy if he could direct him to the bank.

"I will for a dollar," replied the boy.

"Isn't that pretty high?" the man asked.

The boy said, "Not for a bank director."

Chapter 34

Business As Usual

*"Nothing is illegal if a hundred
businessmen decide to do it."*

—*Andrew Young*

☞ A dying farmer told his wife, "I want the businessmen in town to be my pallbearers."
"Why?" she asked. "They were never close friends."
"They've carried me this far," he replied, "so they might as well carry me the rest of the way."

☞ "I want $500,000 insurance on this apartment building," the landlord told his insurance agent.
"Do you want fire insurance or hurricane insurance?" the agent asked.
"Fire insurance, stupid. Who can start a hurricane?"

☞ What's the difference between a mathematician, a statistician and a consultant? Ask each of them what two plus two equals.
The mathematician will tell you the answer is four.
The statistician will say the answer ranges from 3.0 to 4.5.
And the consultant will come up close to you and whisper in your ear, "What would you like it to be?"

☞ Outside city hall, a young lad selling newspapers bellowed, "Extra! Extra! Read all about it! Two men swindled!"
A man walked up to the boy, bought a paper and sat down to read it. "Hey, kid," he yelled. "There's nothing here about two men being fooled."
Just then, he heard the paper boy yelling, "Extra! Extra! Read all about it! Three men swindled!"

☞ The owner of a large business bought a lot of signs with the message, "Do It Now!" and hung them all over the office, hoping to inspire his employees to be energetic and prompt in their daily work.

Soon after, a friend asked him how the experiment was working.

"Well, not exactly as I expected," he said. "The cashier skipped town with $45,000, the head bookkeeper eloped with my secretary and three clerks asked for a raise."

☛ Two businessmen in town were talking. "Is your advertising getting any results?" asked the first.

"I'll say it is," moaned the second. "Last week we advertised for a night watchman and the next night we were robbed."

☛ Three barn builders, one from North Dakota, one from Illinois and one from New York, were at a convention. On the flight home, their plane crashed and they found themselves at the Pearly Gates. When St. Peter found out what they did for a living he was overjoyed.

"You fellows are just in time," he said. "Heaven needs some repairs—our stairway is a little rickety and we could use some new cloud-launching ramps. Why don't each of you give me a bid on what it would cost."

The first contractor, from North Dakota, said it would cost $3,000 for the job. St. Peter asked him to break down the figures so he could understand them.

The North Dakotan said $1,000 was for labor, $1,000 for materials and $1,000 for overhead and profit.

The Illinois contractor's bid was $6,000, with the same breakdown divided into $2,000 chunks.

The contractor from New York turned in his bid. It was for $9,000. St. Peter said it seemed high compared with the others and wanted to know how the Big Apple builder got his figures.

"It's easy, St. Peter," he said. "It comes out to $3,000 for you, $3,000 for me, and we give the guy from North Dakota $3,000 to get the job done."

☛ The exterminator called one of his farm clients. "I'm very sorry to tell you this, Mrs. Lee," he said, "but your check just came back."

"We are even, then," the lady said. "So did those ants you promised me you had driven out of my house forever."

☛ A business executive is a person who can take two hours for lunch without having anybody miss him.

184

☛ Advertising is when the local seed corn dealer puts a sign up next to a cornfield that says a certain high-powered hybrid was planted here.

Public relations is when the dry weather makes the corn look terrible and the hybrid corn salesman goes and takes the sign down.

☛ A farm wife, who had just finished her weekly grocery trip, returned to the checkout counter and said, "You gave me the wrong change."

The checkout girl said, "How long ago did this happen?"

After the woman said it happened about 20 minutes ago, the checkout girl pointed to the sign that read, "All errors in change must be reported at time of checkout or they will not be corrected...Management."

The farm wife said, "You mean I'm too late?"

"I'm afraid so."

"All right," she said, walking out. "Too late is too late. I just wanted you to know you gave me $10 too much change."

☛ A farmer named Mort wrote a note to a fellow poultry farmer that read, "The crate you shipped those hens in was dilapidated. It fell apart while I was bringing it home from the railroad depot and all the hens escaped. I only rounded up 10, so kindly send refund."

A week later, the farmer received a note in the mail that read, "Congratulations, Mort. There were only six hens in that crate. Invoice for additional hens is enclosed."

☛ A cattle feeder died, went to the gates of Heaven and met St. Peter. St. Peter said, "Sorry, but our quota of cattle feeders is filled up right now."

So, the feeder sat down, then stood up and hollered, "Cattle prices were up $5 per cwt. this morning down in Hell!"

Soon, 250 cattle feeders tore out of Heaven and headed down below.

St. Peter walked over and told the cattle feeder there was room for him in Heaven now. But the feeder thought for a moment and said, "No thanks. I'd better go down below and check out those prices—there just might be some truth to that rumor."

☛ A couple of hot air balloonists were cruising over the countryside and had no idea of their location. Finally, they were able to land the balloon in a farm field and hiked out to the road where they spotted a man on a bicycle eyeing the strange-looking apparatus in the field.

"Where are we?" asked one of the balloonists.

"You're in a field," the guy on the bike replied.

The other balloonist then asked, "You don't happen to be an accountant, do you?"

"Why, yes, I am," the bicyclist responded. "How did you know?"

"Well," the balloonist answered, "your answer was absolutely correct, but totally useless."

☛ The owner of a sawmill wanted to buy some timber from a mountain land-owner. The owner was asking top dollar and refused to lower the price.

"Why, old man," the sawmill operator protested, "I can buy timber from the government cheaper than that."

"Maybe so," agreed the mountaineer, "but the government's in debt and I ain't."

☛ A real estate man was using some high pressure tactics to sell a plot of poor farmland to a neighboring farmer. "All this land needs is a little water, a cool breeze and some people to farm it," he said.

"Maybe so," replied the farmer, "but that's all Hell needs too."

Chapter 35

Egads!
Another Salesman!

*"Opportunity knocks sometimes...
but most of the time it's just
another lousy salesman."*

☛ The pushy vacuum cleaner salesman scattered a sack of well-pulverized "barnyard residue" on the rural client's best rug and then said confidently, "Lady, if this marvelous vacuum cleaner won't pick up every particle, I'll eat it."

"Start eating, you fool!" replied the husky housewife. "We don't have electricity."

☛ A sign was posted on the front door of an Arkansas home that read: "We shoot every third salesman, and the second one just left."

☛ A young real estate salesman had just closed his first deal, only to discover the farm he had sold was completely under water.

"My customer's going to come back here mighty mad," he complained to his boss. "Should I give him his money back?"

"Money back?" roared his boss. "What kind of salesman are you? Get out there and sell him a pontoon corn planter!"

☛ A farmer drove away a pesky salesman by yelling, "I can't stand you! I don't like your products! I hate you bothering me! Get off my property now!"

"Man, I wish I had a hundred customers like you," replied the salesman.

"Why?" asked the farmer, a bit surprised by the comment.

"Because," said the salesman, "right now I've got a thousand customers like you."

☞ A television salesman was traveling through a rural community and gave a convincing home demonstration on the latest remote-controlled TV set. He installed the set in the home, then took the remote control a block down the street and switched channels without any difficulty.

A week after the sale, the owner called the salesman and complained about the remote control. "Doesn't it work?" the salesman asked.

"Oh, yes," the customer said. "It works just fine. But it's getting to be quite a nuisance going down the street every time I want to change the channel."

☞ One farm machinery company sales manager agreed with the statement that good salesmen were hard to find. "Last week," he said, "I had to call three bars, two movie houses and a massage parlor just to find one of our guys."

☞ The chief executive officer of a farm supply company made a surprise appearance at the sales manager's door. "Who's our best salesman?" the executive asked.

"That's Dick, sir," the sales manager said. "Last week he sold two milking machines to a farmer who had only one cow—and then took the cow as the down-payment."

☞ Al, a top-notch door-to-door salesman, was telling the rookie salesman about his selling tactics.

"I sell women's hose," Al said. "Sometimes, if the woman of the house is really interested, I put them on for her."

"You must sell plenty that way," replied the wide-eyed rookie.

"No, not really," Al said. "My legs look lousy in women's hose."

☞ It was his second day on the job and the rookie salesman looked depressed.

Snap out of it," said his boss. "Don't look so gloomy. Sure it'll be tough at first, but with a little experience, you'll make sales."

"That's not it," said the new salesman. "When I got home last night I practiced my sales talk on my wife—and now I've got to buy her a vacuum cleaner."

☞ A farmer took his young son out to the town's cemetery one afternoon. The two saw a tombstone with an epitaph that read: "Here lies Roy Kelly, a farm machinery salesman and an honest man."

"Imagine that," said the farmer, "three people buried in one grave."

☞ Is this guy a salesman or what? Last Christmas he convinced his wife polyester is the generic name for mink.

☞ A young farm girl told her friend that she had just become engaged to Larry, a traveling salesman.

"Is Larry handsome?" the friend asked.

"Nope," she said, "he's no beauty."

"Does he have money?"

"If he does, he won't spend it," she said.

"What about bad habits," said the friend. "Does he have any?"

"Well, Larry drinks an awful lot," said the future bride.

"I don't understand," said the friend. "If you can't say anything nice about him, then why are you marrying him?"

"He's on the road all the time," she said. "I'll never see him!"

☞ There was an annoying traveling salesman named Eddie who was disturbing every house in the rural community with his two-hour-long pitches selling sharp knives. It was so bad that some people were buying the knives just to get the pest out of their homes.

But when Eddie knocked at the door of Mrs. Davidson, neighbors were shocked to see him turn around and quickly walk off the property. "How'd you get rid of him?" a neighbor asked. "What's your secret?"

"Oh, it's very simple," Mrs. Davidson explained. "I told him I was so glad he came because I wanted to show him my latest line of greeting cards."

☞ An insurance salesman arrived at a big office building with an appointment to see the company sales manager. He stuck his head in the door and said sheepishly, "Excuse me, sir, but you don't want to buy any insurance, do you?"

The sales manager yelled, "No!" and the insurance salesman turned to walk away.

"Young man, come back here. You'll never make a sale that way," the sales manager said and began lecturing him on the art of salesmanship and the importance of developing sales pitches to fit the needs of the customer.

"What you lack is confidence, son," the sales manager said. "Get out your application blanks. I'll buy some of your insurance to give you confidence."

The application was filled out and the salesman completed the sale. "Now remember what I told you," said the manager, "you use different approaches for each customer."

"I do that," said the salesman.

"What do you mean, you do that?" the surprised sales manager asked.

"Well," he said, "this is my approach for selling to sales managers, and it works almost every time."

☞ It's been said that sales managers really love the circus. It always makes them feel better to know that they're not the only ones with a bunch of clowns on the payroll.

☞ After a convincing sales pitch, a life insurance salesman smiled and handed his client the applications. However, the applicant was having trouble filling out the forms. The salesman asked what the trouble was and the man said that he couldn't answer the question about the cause of death of his father.

The salesman wanted to know why. After some embarrassment, the client explained his father had been hanged.

The salesman scratched his chin for a moment. He said, "Just write: 'Father was taking part in a public function when the platform gave way.'"

☞ An expert salesman is the man who can make his wife feel sorry for the girl who lost her compact in his car.

☞ A fast-talking salesman was trying to sell the farmer a new car. "This car is so fast," he declared, "that if you left here at eight o'clock in the evening, you'd be in Chicago by four in the morning."

"I'll think it over," the farmer said as he left.

The salesman called the farmer the next day and the farmer said, "Look, I've decided not to buy the car—I can't think of any reason why I should be in Chicago at four o'clock in the morning."

☛ The insurance salesman had his prospect on the hook and was about ready to move in for the kill. "Now that amounts," he concluded, "to premiums of $50 per month on a straight life. That's what you want, isn't it?"

"Well," the customer said reluctantly, "I would like to fool around once in a while on Saturday night."

☛ A vacationer at a hunting lodge decided to rent a dog for the weekend. He was given a dog named "Salesman," who was a terrific hunting dog. When the same man returned the following year, he asked for Salesman once again.

"Sorry, he ain't no good anymore," the guide said.

"Why, what happened?"

"We figured he was so good that he deserved a promotion, so we renamed him 'Sales Manager,'" the guide said. "Ever since, all he wants to do is sit on his haunches and growl."

☛ Creative selling is the lumber dealer who calls people up at three o'clock in the morning—and in a real deep voice, tells them to build an ark.

☛ A door-to-door salesman, who wasn't having much luck with his product, tried a new approach. He walked up to the next farm house and said, "Let me show you a little item your neighbors said you couldn't afford."

☛ In a small town, a salesman gave up selling and became a policeman. A friend asked, "How do you like your change from salesman to police officer?"

"Fine," the fellow answered. "The pay is regular and the hours are all right. But what I like best is that the customer is always wrong."

☛ A good salesman is a fellow who can convince his wife that she looks fat in a fur coat.

☛ The salesman's handbook reads: "The most important part of being a salesman is confidence." With today's salesmen, confidence is going after Moby Dick with a rowboat, a harpoon and a jar of tartar sauce!

☛ A salesman's wife was giving a special party and asked her butcher for something really special to serve. He suggested human brains and said there were three kinds:

Farmer brains at $10 per pound, doctor brains at $25 per pound and salesman brains at $75 per pound.

Proudly, the wife asked why salesman brains were so expensive.

"Lady," the butcher said, "did you ever stop to realize how many salesmen you would need to get one pound of brains?"

Government

"American farmers don't need protection from competition to survive. They need protection from their own government."

Your Friends
In Washington

*"I don't make jokes—I just watch
the government and report the facts."*

—*Will Rogers*

☛ The secretary of agriculture and his aides were said to be circling the countryside in a plane when a burst of compassion struck the secretary. "I think I'll just throw this $100 bill out the window and make at least one farmer happy," the ag secretary said.

"Wait, Mr. Secretary," an aide said. "I've got two $50 bills. You could throw them out the window and make two farmers happy."

The pilot, hearing all this, couldn't resist: "Why don't you open the door and all jump out? You'd make everybody happy."

☛ Little Eddie wanted $100 so badly he decided to pray for it. He prayed for several weeks with no results, so he wrote a letter to God.

The post office finally forwarded the letter to the White House. The president chuckled and ordered $5 sent to the boy. The boy, delighted that his prayers had been answered, even if only in part, wrote a thank-you note to God but added a P.S. message: "I noticed you routed my letter through Washington and, as usual, the bureaucrats deducted 95%."

☛ A politician was thrown into the alley by two thugs. One of the robbers put a gun to the politician's head and said, "Give me all your money or I'll blow your brains out!"

The politician thought for a second and answered, "Go ahead and shoot. In my profession I can live without brains, but not without money."

☞ It's rumored that the newest guided missile is going to be named "Civil Service Servant." It won't work, you can't fire it and it's costing the taxpayers a fortune.

☞ Two farmers were griping about Washington bureaucrats. "What do you have when you have three ag economists up to their necks in wet cement?"
His friend shrugged his shoulders. The first farmer chuckled and said, "Not enough cement!"

☞ A Department of Health, Education and Welfare employee, conducting a poll in a rural community, asked a 71-year-old lady, "What do you think of Medicare?"
"I don't know, myself," she replied, "but I have a friend that tried it and lost 21 pounds."

☞ You've got to pity poor George Washington. He couldn't blame his troubles on the previous administration.

☞ A man asked a farmer, "What's your brother Archie doing?"
"Nothing," the farmer replied.
"But I thought he was trying to get a government job."
The farmer said, "He got it."

☞ Old Harold was a legend among the kids in town, who were always rushing to his house to see him. One day, as he sat out on the steps of his house, he was asked by a little girl, "How do I get to Carnegie Hall?"
"Practice! Practice!" Harold said.
Then a little boy asked, "How do I get to the White House?"
Harold advised, "Make promises. Tell lies."

☞ The Lord's Prayer contains 56 words; Lincoln's Gettysburg Address, 260; the Ten Commandments, 300; the Declaration of Independence, 3,000—and a recent government order setting the price of cabbage, 26,911.

☞ You've got to give the president a lot of credit for foresight. Last year he told us to tighten our belts, which was a good thing. Because what's happening now is enough to scare the pants off you.

☞ George Bush traveled to Israel for a meeting with the prime minister. Bush waited for the Israeli prime minister for over an hour and was pretty miffed at his tardiness.

"For gosh sakes, Yitzhak, call me the next time you're running late, will you?" Bush said. "I'm really busy with all the stuff in the Middle East and that Democratic Congress."

The prime minister said he was sorry. "But I just couldn't get away. I was talking to someone more important than you are."

Bush sighed and said, "C'mon. Will you please tell me who is more important than the president of the United States?"

"Moses."

"Moses?" Bush asked. "You were talking to Moses?"

"Sure."

"Hey, get him on the phone for me," Bush said. "I want to talk to him."

The prime minister said he would try. He picked up the phone, dialed, listened and then hung up.

"Well?"

"I'm sorry, Mr. President," the prime minister said. "Moses said the last time he talked to a bush, it cost him 40 years in the wilderness."

☞ Our government is one of checks and balances. The more checks the government writes, the worse the balance gets.

☞ A farmer walked up to a man who was standing at attention in front of the Washington Monument and holding a bugle.

"What on earth are you doing here?" asked the farmer.

"My job is to wait here and sound the bugle when all of the farm groups in the country agree on what we need in the way of farm policy," the man said.

"How much do you get paid?" the farmer asked.

"$3.75 per hour."

"That's not very much," the farmer said.

"I know," the man said, "but you have to remember this is a lifetime job."

☞ Congress acted wisely when it voted for the recent increase in minimum wage. They didn't want anyone to have to work more than an hour to make the money to buy a gallon of gas.

☛ A farm family visiting Washington rounded the corner onto a downtown street and looked up and down both sides of the street, puzzled. Approaching a policeman, the wife asked, "Which side is the State Department on?"

After a moment's hesitation, the policeman replied, "Ours, I think."

☛ A Washington bureaucrat, who had served during several administrations, was telling a friend about his house. "It's an old Georgetown house," he said, "and it would probably crumble to the ground if it weren't held together by old FBI wiring."

☛ Let's face it, if the Ten Commandments had been written up as Federal regulations and issued on stone—Moses would not have come down from Mount Sinai with two tablets. He would have come down with a hernia.

☛ A farmer's look at government:

Communism: You have two cows. The government takes both of them and gives you part of the milk.

Socialism: You have two cows. The government takes one and gives it to your neighbor.

Fascism: You have two cows. The government takes both cows and sells you the milk.

Nazism: You have two cows. The government takes both cows, then shoots you.

Capitalism: You have two cows. You sell one of them and buy a bull.

Bureaucracy: You have two cows. The government takes both of them, shoots one, milks the other, then pours the milk down the drain.

☛ One farmer was overheard saying, "I finally found one thing I have in common with my son. He listens to rock groups, and I listen to ag economists—and neither one of us understands a word they're saying."

☛ Glenn, the owner of a small crossroads store, was appointed postmaster. Over six months went by and not one piece of mail left town.

Deeply concerned, postal authorities in Washington wrote Glenn to inquire why. They received this short and simple explanation: "The bag ain't full yet."

☞ Yuri, a Russian diplomat, was describing Soviet life to American politicians. "Yes," he said, "Russian politics aren't so bad, except for the time many years ago when I was sent to prison in Siberia."

"What happened?" they asked.

"On election day, I was handed a sealed envelope to drop in the box," Yuri explained. "I began to tear it open when a Soviet official shouted, 'What do you think you are doing?'"

Yuri explained to the official that he wanted to see for whom he was voting.

"Then, the official said, 'Are you crazy? This is a secret ballot!' and they carried me off," Yuri said.

☞ The only time one of us would want to be president is around the first of the month when we would like to veto a few bills.

☞ The Russian political leader, while visiting the U.S., was being interviewed and a reporter asked if he objected to jokes that were being told.

"Not at all," he replied. "I like jokes about myself."

The reporter then asked if he heard many jokes. The Russian president thought for a moment and said, "Enough to fill three or four labor camps."

☞ "What are you smiling at?" Noah asked his wife as their giant boat rocked over the waves.

"I was just thinking," replied his wife, "how lucky it was we could go ahead and build this ark without waiting for an appropriation from Congress."

☞ This could mean trouble. The vice president just walked into the Oval Office and said, "Play me or trade me."

☞ A Washington farm reporter returned to the office and said, "I've got the perfect news story."

His editor asked, "What is it? Man bites dog?"

"No," the reporter replied, "bull throws senator."

☞ Only a politician would ask you to buy a ticket to a $100-a-plate dinner and then give a speech on how he intends to stop inflation.

☛ A rural plumber who wanted to clean a large amount of iron pipe wrote a government agency asking if he should use hydrochloric acid. In due course, he received a letter written in government jargon, ending with the phrase: "Be advised that hydrochloric acid is deleterious to the substance in question."

The confused plumber wrote his thanks and added that he was ordering the acid immediately. A few days later, he got a special delivery letter from the same agency, written in the same mumbo jumbo, and ending: "The usage of hydrochloric acid is definitely contraindicated."

Again, he wrote his thanks and said he would use the acid as soon as it arrived. The next day he got a telegram: "Don't use it. It'll eat the hell out of your pipes."

☛ One man's definition of federal aid: It is like giving yourself a transfusion by drawing blood from the right arm, returning it to the left arm—and spilling 90 percent on the way across.

☛ Grandpa observes that freedom is being able to do whatever you want to do without having to answer to anyone except your wife, the police, the state, federal and city authorities and your neighbors.

☛ Once upon a time there was an ant who worked hard all day in the fields. It was summer and the ant was busy cutting grass and dragging it home.

The ant had a grasshopper for a neighbor. The grasshopper lived on welfare and sat in his doorway singing all day. When winter came, the ant had a whole bale of grass.

But the ant had violated the Federal Farm Law for overharvesting grass. He was fined $162.50 and the surplus was seized. The grasshopper received the surplus in exchange for his food stamps.

☛ A rural Utah teacher told a boy in class that he would never grow up to be president, but with his absentee record, he might make it to the Senate.

☛ A Native American Indian reportedly sent a note to the president. Included was the short message: "Be careful with your new immigration laws. We were careless with ours."

☞ At a communist meeting, one of the attending comrades suddenly stood up during the debate and addressed the chairman.

"Comrade Speaker," he said. "There's just one thing I want to know. What happens to my unemployment compensation checks when we overthrow the government?"

☞ A guide at the Grand Canyon told a group of touring farmers, "It took millions of years to carve this out."

One of the farmers turned to his wife and said, "It must have been a government project."

☞ Two farmers were sipping on lemonade on the front porch. "What's wrong about four politicians riding in a Cadillac that misses the turn and runs off a cliff?" Ike asked.

"I don't know," said the other. "What?"

Ike chuckled, "It seats eight."

☞ An old farmer was driving a truck along the highway and was speeding. A state trooper flagged him down and said, "Do you realize you were going 80 miles per hour?"

"No, I didn't," the farmer said.

"Haven't you got a governor on that truck?" the trooper asked.

"No, sir," said the farmer. "The governor's in the state Capitol—that's fertilizer you smell."

☞ Down-on-his-luck Murray said things have really picked up since the new president took office. They've picked up his television, his washing machine and if he doesn't pay up, they said they're going to pick up his refrigerator.

☞ Three kids at summer camp were bragging about whose father was the fastest. The farm boy said, "My dad is so fast that he can shoot an arrow at a target and then run and catch the arrow before it hits."

The feed salesman's son bragged, "That's nothing. My dad can shoot his pistol, pick up a target, run to the end of the range and put it up before the bullet gets there."

The ag economist's boy thought a minute and then replied, "My dad's got you all beat. He works for the government and gets off work at 4:30 p.m., but he's always home by 3:45."

Chapter 37

A Kiss For The Baby...

"Politicians are the same all over. They promise to build a bridge even when there's no river."

—*Nikita Krushchev*

☛ A famous magician arrived in town and decided to visit the local tavern.

When a farmer asked the stranger what he did for a living, the magician rambled, "My act is sensational! I trick millions of people a year. I make a big production from nothing and then cause hundreds of dollar bills to completely vanish into thin air!"

The farmer, a bit confused, asked the man, "So what are you, a magician or a U.S. senator?"

☛ A building contractor wanted to give a politician a sports car to convince him to send a high-budgeted deal his way. The politician objected and said, "Sir, common decency and my sense of honor would never permit me to accept a gift like that."

"I understand," the contractor said, smirking. "Suppose we do this. I'll sell you the sports car for $10."

The politician thought for a moment or two. "In that case," he said, "I'll take two."

☛ As an irritated candidate was being heckled, he exclaimed, "There seem to be a great many fools here tonight. I wonder if it would be possible to hear one at a time."

"That's fair enough," shouted a man seated in the middle. "Finish your speech."

☛ It's no wonder that politicians work so hard to get re-elected. They know they can't make it in private business with all the laws they pass.

☛ A little girl asked her mother if all fairy tales began with "Once upon a time."

Her mother replied, "No, dear. Nowadays most of them begin with, 'If I'm elected...'"

☛ A campaign manager in Texas called his congressional candidate and said urgently, "Jim, you've got to come to Houston. They're telling lies about you here."

"I can't today," the candidate said. "It's worse in Dallas. They're telling the truth about me there!"

☛ Once upon a time there was a beautiful young woman who found a frog in a flooded field. The frog was so grateful he started talking. "I was once a rich politician. Kiss me and I'll turn back into one."

The woman immediately popped the frog into her purse. Why? A talking frog is worth a lot more than a politician.

☛ After speaking, the campaigning senator approached a farmer in the crowd and asked, "Well, what did you think of my speech?"

The farmer answered, "It was OK, but it reminds me of a longhorn steer."

"Oh, how's that?"

"Well," said the farmer, "you have a strong point on each side and a lot of bull in the middle."

☛ While touring a third-world country in Africa, a politician was captured by a cannibal. The man-eater boasted to his tribe, "I've captured a politician!"

The statement barely drew a response. "So what?" the chief asked.

"Well," the man said, "now I can try a baloney sandwich."

☛ "I need a job, Senator," insisted Merle, a voter from the lawmaker's home town.

The senator thought for a moment. "Well, I'll tell you, Merle," he said, "there aren't any jobs available. But here's what I'll do. I'll start up a committee to investigate why there aren't any jobs. And you can head that committee."

☛ Two farmers were discussing the election for mayor. "What do you think of the two candidates, Floyd?"

Floyd thought for a while and answered, "Well, all I can tell you is that I'm glad only one can get elected."

☛ At the debate, a voter was offered $10 to vote for the Democrats in the election. He was then offered $20 to vote Republican. He ended up voting for the Democrats because they were less corrupt.

☛ A politician was addressing a large group of voters when the microphone suddenly went dead. Raising his voice, the politician shouted to a man in the back row, "Can you hear me?"

The man cupped his ear and shook his head 'no.'

Seeing this, a man in the front row stood up and shouted to the gent in the back, "Well, I can hear from here and I'd be happy to change places with you."

☛ A working definition of a politician: Someone who not only put the cart before the horse, but also put the cart ahead of the wheel.

☛ Farmer Burt suddenly died and appeared at St. Peter's Pearly Gates when the saint asked him if he wished to enter Heaven.

After Burt said that he did indeed, St. Peter said, "Then you must suffer a bit more before I can allow you to enter, for your life as a farmer was not exactly immaculate. You must spend one month with the ugliest, stupidest woman on earth."

"What?" Burt replied. "I don't know about this, let me think it over."

Just then, Burt saw Dick, his hometown's mayor, floating on a cloud with a gorgeous blonde.

"Hey," Burt called to St. Peter, "that's not fair. I've led a much better life than that crook and he gets to be with a beautiful woman."

"Relax," St. Peter said. "You've got it all wrong—that's her punishment."

☛ Both mayoral candidates happened to sit next to each other at the diner one afternoon. Trying to outdo his opponent, one candidate said, "I always tip the waitresses really well and then ask them to vote for me."

His opponent answered, "I always tip them five cents—and then ask them to vote for you."

☞ The key to being a successful politician is finding out where the public is going, taking a shortcut across the field, getting out in front and making them think you're leading the way.

☞ Two men were opposing each other for a political office. One angrily said to his opponent, "Did you tell Jake down at the barbershop that I'm a thieving, lying shyster?"

"No," the other candidate said. "I don't know how he found out."

☞ You're an old-timer if you remember when the only babes politicians kissed were those in their mother's arms.

☞ The congressman seeking spiritual advice from the church was advised by the bishop to go out in the rain and lift his head toward Heaven. "It will bring a revelation to you," he promised.

The congressman reported back the next day and said, "I followed your advice and no revelation came. The water poured down my neck and I felt like a fool."

"Well," said the bishop, "that's quite a revelation for the first try, isn't it?"

☞ On the electric hand dryer in a city hall restroom was scribbled, "For a message from our mayor, kindly press button."

☞ Annoyed by a local politician, a farmer said to the candidate, "I wouldn't vote for you if you were St. Peter!"

"If I were St. Peter," said the candidate, "you couldn't vote for me because you wouldn't be in my district."

☞ What's the difference between a statesman and a politician? A statesman is working for the public, while the politician has the public working for him.

☞ A farm mother was making dinner when she looked out the window to see her two boys completely covered with mud. "You kids stop throwing mud at each other!" she hollered. "Are you having a fight?"

"No, Ma," one of her sons answered. "We're just playing politics."

☛ A politician who had radically changed his platform was congratulated by a colleague. "I'm glad you've seen the light," he told the politician.

"I didn't see the light," he said. "I felt the heat."

☛ "Let me tell you, ladies and gentlemen, it is the working classes that have made this country what it is today," the candidate said to a rural audience as he hesitated, expecting applause.

Instead, an angry farmer shouted, "That's the way with you politicians, blame everything on the poor folks!"

☛ At the candidate's speech in town, he bragged, "I've now been elected three times!"

A farmer's voice was heard from the rear. "Yeah, and they'll keep electing you 'till you learn your job!"

☛ It is said you can fool all of the people some of the time, but you can't fool all of the people all of the time. On the other hand, it does give candidates something to aim at.

☛ A banker, electrician and politician were all taking an IQ test. One of the questions was:

"What term would you use to describe the problem that results when the outflow exceeds the inflow?"

The banker wrote, "Overdraft."

The electrician wrote, "Overload."

And the politician wrote, "What problem?"

☛ One of the biggest jobs politicians face is getting money from taxpayers without disturbing the voters.

☛ Jerome came home from the county sheriff election and told his wife, "Honey, I've just been elected!"

"Honestly?" his wife asked, surprised.

Jerome frowned and said, "Now why'd you have to bring that up?"

☛ It was rumored that one state politician hired two research assistants—one to dig up the facts and the other to bury them.

☛ A new reporter had been assigned to cover upcoming local elections and asked a veteran newsman how one could tell whether a politician was lying.

"That's easy, kid," the old-timer laughed. "Just watch his body language. If he touches his hair, he's telling the truth. If he scratches his nose, he's telling the truth. But if he opens his mouth..."

☛ A seedy-looking man sitting in the first row at the mayoral election speeches was bothering the mayor with his loud outbursts of laughter. Finally, the incumbent mayor pointed to the heckler and said, "Will that gentleman who differed with me please get up and tell the audience what he has done for the good of the city?"

The bum stood up and the mayor persisted, saying, "Speak up, tell this audience just one way in which you have ever tried to help this city."

"Well, Mr. Mayor," said the man in a loud, firm voice, "I voted against you in the last election."

☛ One of the two candidates for judge in a small community was notorious for his dishonesty. Talking about the elections with her neighbor, a farm wife was asked why she was going to vote for the dishonest man, since his opponent was a man of unquestioned integrity.

"I look at it this way," she explained. "If a man isn't ruined when he goes into office, he's ruined when he comes out. And there isn't any use in ruining a perfectly good man."

☛ A surgeon, an engineer and a politician were debating which of their professions was the oldest.

"Eve was made from Adam's rib," said the surgeon, "and that, of course, was a surgical procedure."

"Yes," countered the engineer, "but before that, order was created out of chaos—and that most certainly was an engineering job."

"Ah-ha!" exclaimed the politician triumphantly. "And just who do you think created the chaos?"

Chapter 38

Tax Attacks

*"Auditors are the people
who go in after the war is lost
and bayonet the wounded."*

—*P. Rubin*

☞ A young child swallowed a dime in a store and his frightened mother called for help. A stranger promptly seized the child by the heels, gave him a few shakes and the coin rolled out on the floor.

The grateful mother thanked the stranger and asked, "Are you a doctor?"

"No, ma'am," he replied. "I work for the Internal Revenue Service."

☞ The rural pastor received a call from an I.R.S. agent inquiring about a $5,000 contribution claimed by a member of the parish. The investigator asked, "Did Mr. Roberts give that amount?"

The pastor thought to himself for a moment and then replied, "I really cannot say just now, but if you'll check back with me tomorrow, I'm sure the answer will be yes."

☞ A farmer was talking to his hired hand, "I really don't understand why the I.R.S. doesn't serve coffee and dough-nuts," he said. "The Red Cross does when they take your blood."

☞ 365 days in the year
You work like the devil to make it
And just when you're ready
To start eating steady
The government's ready to take it.

☞ When the pioneers settled this country hundreds of years ago, the Indians were running it. There were no taxes, no national debt and the women did all the work. And these guys thought they could improve the system?

☞ Conscience is the small voice inside your head that tells you the I.R.S. might check your return this year.

☞ A farmer was called in by the I.R.S. to explain a deduction. He was disputing the rule that a baby born in January could not be entered as a deduction on the previous year's tax schedule.
"Why not?" the cross farmer asked. "It was last year's business."

☞ Golf and income taxes have a lot in common. You drive hard for the green, but end up in the hole.

☞ Two farmers, an American and a Dutchman were talking. "What does your flag look like?" asked the American.
"It has three stripes—red, white and blue," the Dutchman replied. "We say they have a connection with our taxes—we get red when we talk about them, white when we get our tax bills and we pay them until we're blue in the face."
The American replied, "With us, we see stars, too!"

☞ There are two kinds of taxpayers. First, the ones who hope the government will do something for them, and second, the ones who hope the government won't do anything to them.

☞ A revenue man stopped a little mountain lad and offered him $1 if he took him to his dad's still.
"OK," the boy said, "but I want the money in advance."
"Oh, no," the man said, "not until you point it out."
"Look here," the boy countered. "If I take you to my old man's still, you ain't coming back."

☞ The United States of America is the only country where it takes more time and brains to make out the income tax return than it does to make the income.

☞ "And now, ladies and gentleman," said the campaigning U.S. senator, "I wish to tax your memory."

"Good heavens," muttered his colleague, "why haven't we thought of that before?"

☞ A taxpayer is one who doesn't have to pass a civil service examination to work for the government.

☞ Old Milo did his best again this year to write everything possible off on his tax forms. One day, an angry I.R.S. agent called and asked the farmer, "What do you mean writing off your tax payments to the government from last year, claiming it was a poor investment?"

☞ Congress does some strange things. It puts a high tax on liquor and then it raises other taxes so much that it drives people to drink.

☞ A dusty, shrewd-looking man jumped out of his car outside the farmer's house. "Fine piece of land out here!" he exclaimed.

"You're right, there," the farmer replied eagerly. "It's the best to be found in the county."

"What's land worth out here?"

"It's worth every penny of $600 an acre," answered the farmer with an eye to business. "You thinking of settling in these parts?"

"Hardly," said the stranger as he made some notes in a book. "I'm Herbert, the new tax assessor."

☞ Just about the time a fellow is cured of swearing, it's time to file another income tax return.

☞ A successful farm machinery dealer was on his deathbed. He summoned his best friend and made him promise to see that his mortal remains would be cremated.

The friend agreed, but cautiously asked, "What would you want me to do with the ashes?"

"Place them in an envelope," gasped the dying man, "and send them to the Collector of Internal Revenue and tell him: 'Now you have everything.'"

Chapter 39

You're In
The Army Now

*"You can have peace. Or you
can have freedom. Don't ever
count on having both at once."*
—Robert Heinlein

☛ "Well," growled the tough old sergeant to the private from
the country, "I suppose after you get your discharge from the
Army you'll just be waiting for me to die so you can come and
spit on my grave."

"Not me, Sarge," the soldier assured him. "Once I get out
of this Army, I ain't never going to stand in line again!"

☛ Two farm boys who had never been far from home
enlisted in the army and were on their way overseas. As their
ship left the harbor, they stared in amazement at a light-
house.

"I'll be darned, Billy," said his brother, "isn't that one heck
of a place to put a silo!"

☛ The mess sergeant was tired of hearing the men complain
about his cooking. "I don't know why you guys gripe about
this bread. The boys at Valley Forge would have loved to have
had it."

"Sure they would," a private piped up. "It was fresh then."

☛ A young farm boy breezed into the recruiting station one
day and announced he wanted to enlist.

"Do you want a commission?" the recruiting officer asked.

"No thanks," the farm boy replied. "I'm such a lousy shot
that I'd be better off working on a straight salary."

☛ A kid from the country was drafted into the Army. When he appeared before the enlistment officer, he was asked what he thought about Communists.

"I hate 'em," the kid replied. "I'd kill every last one of them. I'd stab 'em, shoot 'em, bayonet 'em. If they took all my weapons, I'd bite 'em."

Astonished, the officer said, "You sound like you're nuts!"

"Write that down, write that down," the kid said.

☛ The colonel spotted a cigarette butt on the barracks floor during inspection and bellowed at a new recruit, "Is that yours, soldier?"

"Not at all, sir," the kid replied. "Go ahead, you saw it first."

☛ During the war, a bright young farmer in the Army overseas received a letter from his wife wanting to know how she was going to plant the potatoes in the east 40 acres without help.

The soldier wrote back, "Whatever you do, don't dig up the east 40. That's where the guns are buried."

As is customary in wartime, his letter was read by the censor. Not long after, he received a reply from his upset young wife saying, "A company of soldiers overran the east 40 and dug it all up. What should I do now?"

He replied with a short note saying, "Plant the potatoes!"

☛ It's a mistake not to allow women to go into combat. After all, why let all those years of marriage go to waste?

☛ The hillbilly and a city boy had adjoining bunks in the Army. The city soldier was inspecting his toilet kit. Suddenly, he asked, "Hey, Jim Bob, did you take my toothpaste?"

"No, I didn't," replied the hillbilly. "I don't need toothpaste. My teeth ain't loose at all."

☛ A young fellow from the farm was called by the draft board and was given a physical by a doctor who also happened to be the family doctor. He passed easily and was put in the Army, which burned him up.

When he returned home, he stormed into his doctor's office. "You're a fine doctor," he said. "It's funny how you always found something the matter with me when I was paying you $20 a visit!"

☛ The young Army cook had just whipped up orders of fried eggs for a hungry mob of soldiers. Wearied by his efforts, he sat down, yawned, lit a big black cigar and wrote to his sweetheart.

"Darling," he began, "for the past three hours shells have been bursting all around me."

☛ The drill sergeant barked out a command, "All you dummies fall out!"

With much confusion and clatter every man in the company except one fell out and took off. The sergeant glared at the remaining recruit and hollered, "Well?"

The rookie smiled and replied, "There sure were a lot of them, weren't there, Sarge?"

☛ Albert was a young sailor with a speech impediment. However, the Navy officers found that if Albert sang instead of trying to talk, he could communicate much better.

One day on the ship, Albert was so excited he couldn't get the words out. The officer whom he was trying to address grew impatient and shouted, "Sing it, sailor, sing it!"

Albert drew a deep breath and sang:
"Should auld acquaintance be forgot
And never brought to mind?
The Admiral's fallen overboard,
An' he's half a mile behind!"

☛ One of the Army recruits was kind of odd. He walked around the base and if he saw a piece of paper on the ground, he'd pick it up, look at both sides and say, "That's not it!" and then throw it away.

He'd been doing this for months when the Army brass noticed it and thought he might be dangerous to the rest of the men.

They decided to give him an honorable discharge and handed him the signed document.

He looked at it, read both sides and said, "That's it!"

☛ Burning draft cards is a kind of cookout for draft dodgers. It's called chicken barbecue.

☛ Walking through the mess hall, the sergeant stopped and said, "Soldier, I heard you complaining about finding sand in your soup."

The private answered, "That's right, sarge."

"Did you join the Army to serve your country or to complain about the food?" asked the sergeant.

"I joined the Army to serve my country," the private answered, "not to eat it."

☞ The teacher was trying to impress upon her class the advantages of peace and disarmament. "How many of you object to war?" she asked.

Up went several hands. "OK, Peter, tell us why you object to war," she said.

"'Cause wars make history," replied Peter.

☞ The cavalry recruit was instructed to bridle and saddle a horse. Ten minutes later the sergeant major came along and found the recruit holding the bit close to the horse's head.

"What are you waiting for?" he roared.

"Until he yawns," answered the recruit.

☞ Two farm boys were being interviewed for the Navy and were asked, "Do you know how to swim?"

They both looked puzzled and one of them replied, "What's the matter? Aren't there enough ships?"

☞ The sergeant tossed the Army garb at the young country boy and told him to try everything on. When the boy walked out, the sergeant yelled hastily, "Does the uniform fit?"

The recruit answered timidly, "Well, the jacket isn't bad, but the trousers are loose around the armpits."

☞ "Here's a special message from the admiral, Captain Dalton," reported the sailor. "It's marked 'personal.'"

"Read it to me," the captain snapped.

The sailor read: "Of all the blundering, stupid, idiotic morons, Captain Dalton, you take the cake!"

The captain quickly barked, "Have that decoded at once!"

☞ "Gee, Mom," 18-year-old boy complained. "None of the other guys are wearing lipstick!"

"Be quiet, stupid!" she said, twisting his ear. "We're almost at the draft board."

☛ A scientist invented a potion to bring inanimate objects to life. He secretly tried it out on the statue of a general in the park.

Sure enough, the general gave a quiver and climbed down from the pedestal. The scientist was overjoyed. "Tell me, General," he asked, "what's the first thing you're going to do in your new life?"

"That's easy," rasped the general, jerking a gun from his holster. "I'm going to shoot several thousand of these pigeons."

Crime
& Punishment

*"Nobody ever made a law
that could prevent a man
from making a fool of himself."*

Chapter 40

Repeat Offenders

"Some folks commit a crime and go to jail; others commit a crime, write a book and get rich."

☛ The judge looked over his bench and said to the suspect, "You can let me try your case or be tried by a jury of your peers."

"What do you mean, peers?" he asked.

The judge explained, "Peers are men of your own kind— your equals."

"Well," the suspect said, "I sure don't wanna be tried by no bank robbers!"

☛ A farmer was being drilled at the witness stand by the opposing attorney. "At the scene of the accident, did you tell the sheriff you never felt better in your life?"

"Yes, that's right," the farmer said.

"Well, then," the attorney followed, "how is it that you are now claiming you were seriously injured when my client's car hit your wagon?"

"When the sheriff arrived, he went over to my horse, who had a broken leg, and shot him," the farmer said. "Then he went over to Rover, my dog, who was all banged up, and shot him. When he asked me how I felt, I just thought that under the circumstances, it was a wise decision to say I'd never felt better in my life."

☛ Before sentencing, the judge asked the defendant, "Do you challenge any of the jury?"

"Well," he said, "I think I could lick that little fellow on the end."

☛ A social worker visited the small town jail. She asked a dejected man in one cell, "Was it your love of liquor that brought you here?"

"Gosh, no, lady," he answered. "You can't get nothing in here."

☞ Two farmers were talking at the drug store. "What makes you think Sam's so stupid?" Joe asked.

"Well," Art explained, "there's a poster down at the post office that says, 'Man wanted for robbery in Montreal' and Sam packed his bags and applied for the job!"

☞ Judge Brady looked down from the bench and noticed an all-too-familiar figure in handcuffs. "It seems to me that you've been in this court a good many times in the past 20 years," he said sternly.

"I have, your honor," replied the defendant, "and I'm kind of disappointed in you. I figured by now you'd be governor."

☞ "Are you the defendant in this case?" the judge asked.

"No, your honor," he said. "I got a lawyer to do my defending. I'm the one who stole the chickens."

☞ A man charged with murder bribed a friend on the jury to hold out for a verdict of manslaughter. The jury was out for a long period of time, but at last brought in a manslaughter verdict.

Upon visiting the prisoner the following week, the friend was thanked. "You must have had a tough time getting them to vote for manslaughter," the prisoner said.

"Tough is right," replied the friend. "The other 11 wanted to acquit you."

☞ The warden approached the condemned prisoner and said, "Now, Gordo, I'll allow you five minutes of grace before your execution."

Gordo answered, "Well, that's not very long, but bring her in."

☞ Two farmers were in a rural convenience store when a hoodlum rushed in waving a gun. "This is a holdup!" he shouted.

While the other patrons were being searched for valuables, one farmer nudged the other. "Take this," he whispered.

"Take what?" hissed his friend.

"The $25 I owe you."

☞ A country boy was in court for fighting. The judge asked him to tell his side of the story.

"Well, Judge," said the boy, "I was in a telephone booth talking to my girl, Sally, when this guy came along and wanted to use the phone. Before I knew what was going on, he grabbed me by the neck and threw me out."

"I take it that was when you got angry," said the judge.

"Well, I got pretty sore," the boy said. "But what made me really mad was when he grabbed my girl and threw her out, too."

☞ "How could you swindle people who trusted you?" the judge scolded the slick con man.

"Your honor," the con man explained, "it's almost impossible to swindle people who don't trust you."

☞ When a mine operator found the combination of his office safe had jammed, he called the warden at the nearby state prison and asked whether any of his inmates would know how to open it.

Twenty minutes later, a convict accompanied by a prison guard showed up. The inmate twiddled the dials a few moments, then calmly opened the door.

"What do you figure I owe you?" asked the mine operator.

"Well," said the convict, "last time I opened a safe like this one, I got $1,800!"

☞ A prisoner, about to be executed before a firing squad, was blindfolded. The captain of the execution squad asked him if he'd like one last cigarette.

"No thanks," said the prisoner, "I'm trying to quit."

☞ A security guard at a local feed mill stopped an employee who was leaving with a large, suspicious-looking bag in a wheelbarrow. "What have you got in there, Smith?" he asked.

"Just sawdust and wood chips," replied Smith.

"I wasn't born yesterday," the guard barked. "Open it up." He dug through the bag, but sure enough, it contained only sawdust and wood chips.

The same thing happened day after day. Each time, the guard would empty the bag and dig through the sawdust, getting all dirty in the process. And each time, he would find nothing.

Finally, he gave in. "Listen, Smith, I know you're up to something, and it's driving me crazy," he said. "I promise to never bother you again if you'll just tell me what you're stealing!"

"Wheelbarrows, my friend, wheelbarrows," smirked Smith.

☞ A man arrested for gambling came before the judge. "We weren't playing for money," Pete explained to the judge. "We were just playing for chips."

"Chips are just the same as money," the judge sternly replied. "I fine you $20."

Pete looked sad, then slowly reached into his pocket and handed the judge four red chips.

☞ A little boy gazed intently at the "wanted" posters on the post office wall. Finally, he turned to his mother and said, "I just don't see why they don't keep these guys when they take their pictures."

☞ Old farmer Elwood was brought before the judge on a speeding charge and was requested to take the oath, "Do you solemnly swear to tell the truth, the whole truth and nothing but the truth?"

Reluctantly, Elwood agreed.

"Now, Elwood, what do you have to say for yourself?" asked the judge.

"Well, judge," he unhappily drawled, "with all them limitations on me, I haven't got a thing to say."

☞ Matt and Pat were caught rustling cattle over the border and after a summary trial, both were sentenced to a hanging.

When the boys strung up Matt, the rope slipped and he fell into the river below, rapidly swimming around a curve and making his escape.

Chagrined, the posse turned to string up Pat, who cautioned them. "Boys, be sure ya tie a better knot this time," he said. "I can't swim a stroke."

☞ Mark and his buddies from the dorm hopped in his car and drove down to Florida for spring break. On only their second day there, they were all thrown behind bars for raising hell.

In the police station, Mark, who was a pre-law student, stood on his legal rights to make one phone call. A short while after he was taken back to his cell, the sergeant stormed back to the cell and hollered, "Who ordered the pizza?"

☛ The judge said, "I'm going to give your wife $300 a month for alimony and child support."

"That's mighty nice of you, your honor," the happy husband said. "From time to time, I'll try to give her a little myself."

☛ Twelve-year-old Gilbert was caught shoplifting after he swiped a candy bar. The police came, took him to the precinct and put him in a cell next to one containing a hardened criminal. When Gilbert told the man he was arrested for stealing a candy bar, the prisoner ridiculed him.

"Listen, kid, you'll never get rich stealing candy," he said. "You've got to do something big, something important. Why don't you rob a bank?"

"I can't," said Gilbert. "I don't get home from school until 4:30."

☛ "Just what good have you done for humanity?" the judge asked the repeat offender before passing sentence.

"Well, your honor," he replied, "I've kept four detectives working steadily for the past ten years."

Chapter 41

Legal Eagles

"Some lawyers are just the opposite of laundrymen—they lose your suit and take you to the cleaners."

☛ When the jury failed to reach a verdict in the cut-and-dried case, the disgusted judge said, "I discharge this jury!"

Immediately, an irate jury member called out, "You can't do that!"

"And why not?" asked the judge.

"Because you didn't hire me," said the juror, pointing to the lawyer for the defense. "He did!"

☛ The divorce lawyer said to her female client, "I'm sorry, but I haven't succeeded in reaching a settlement with your husband that would be eminently fair to both of you."

"Fair to both? Huh!" the woman shouted. "I could have done that myself! What do you think I hired a lawyer for?"

☛ An old-timer was brought in to testify in a slander suit involving two of his neighbors. "Tell me the exact conversation," said the attorney.

"I can't remember it all," answered the witness, "except each one was callin' the other what they both is."

☛ The defense lawyer was talking to his client, a manager from the local farmer's co-op. "I think we'll win the case—I just sent the judge a big bribe," he said.

"You fool!" replied the manager. "Everyone knows that judge is a strict adherent to the law!"

"I know," responded the lawyer. "I sent the bribe in the prosecuting attorney's name."

☛ We should all be grateful for lawyers. Lawyers are the people who get us out of all the trouble we never would have gotten into if it hadn't been for lawyers in the first place.

☛ A first grader slipped and fell on the playground, skinning his knee. The teacher urged him to be brave about it. "Remember, big boys don't cry."

"Cry?" the youngster exclaimed. "I'm not going to cry. I'm going to sue."

☛ The hit-and-run driver was brought to trial. His lawyer pleaded eloquently and at great length on his behalf.

"Your honor," he concluded, "the plaintiff must have been walking very carelessly. My client is a very careful driver. He has been driving for 20 years."

"Your honor," the counsel for the plaintiff interrupted, "if experience is an argument, my client should win this case. He has been walking for 45 years."

☛ Whoever said talk is cheap never hired a lawyer.

☛ A newly-appointed judge was not familiar with the community's legal code and when a bootlegger appeared before him, he was at a loss as to what to fine him. He called up the old justice.

"I've got a bootlegger here," he said. "What should I give him?"

The old judge answered, "Don't give him over $5.00 a quart. I never did."

☛ When the case was called in criminal court, the judge discovered the defendant charged with stealing a farmer's chickens was on hand but without a lawyer. As was his duty, the judge appointed an attorney to defend the accused. It happened that the appointee was an ambitious young fellow who had just graduated from law school.

"Just go into the back room there," the judge told the young lawyer, "and give him the best advice you can."

After 20 minutes, the judge grew impatient and walked into the room to find the young lawyer sitting alone. "Where's your client?" asked the judge.

"Your honor," replied the lawyer, "you said to give him the best advice I knew, and after listening to his story, I thought the best thing he could do was jump out the window and get as far away as he could."

☞ Do you know why attorneys are buried 20 feet under the ground? Because deep down, you know there has to be some good in them.

☞ A farmer was overheard telling his lawyer, "My wife is suing me for divorce. See that she gets it."

☞ An attorney and his client were conferring in the client's cell. "Now, Jake," the lawyer told the accused, "to help me in getting you acquitted, your wife will have to put on a good act in the courtroom. She should dress soberly, look worried and sad, and maybe cry a little."

"That ought to be easy," Jake replied. "All you have to do is tell her I'm going to be acquitted."

☞ The little old lady being examined for jury duty in a small country town was asked if she knew the defense lawyer.

"Yes," she snapped, "he's a crook."

"And the plaintiff's lawyer?"

"Yes—he's a crook, too."

With that the judge called both lawyers over for a conference. He whispered, "If you ask her if she knows me, I'll hit both of you with contempt of court."

☞ A good lawyer is one who knows the law; a clever one takes the judge to lunch.

☞ After waiting two hours in court for his case to be called, one defendant was irked when the judge said, "Court's adjourned. People whose cases haven't been called will have to come back tomorrow."

"What for?" he snapped irritably.

"Contempt of court! I fine you $20. That's why!" roared the judge.

Noticing that the man was checking his wallet, the judge relented somewhat. "That's all right," he said. "You don't have to pay the fine right now."

"Thanks," snapped the defendant, "but I was just checking to see if I have enough to say two more words!"

Chapter 42

Our Flat-Footed Friends

"I have never seen a situation so dismal that a policeman couldn't make it worse."

—Brendan Behan

☛ A frightened old man reported to the police that he'd been struck down in the dark outside his back door by an unknown assailant.

A young policeman was sent to investigate and soon returned to headquarters with a lump on his forehead and a glum look on his face.

"I solved the case," he muttered.

"Amazingly fast work," the police chief said. "How did you accomplish it?"

The young cop explained, "I stepped on the rake, too."

☛ A traffic cop hailed down a speeding automobile. "You were going 90 in a 50 miles per hour zone," said the officer.

"So what?" came the reply. "It's a free country, isn't it?"

"Let's see your driver's license," said the policeman.

"Never had one, I can drive just as well without it," the man said.

"How are your brakes?"

"They're rotten," he said.

"That's three charges against you," the policeman said. "I'm going to have to arrest you."

At that point the driver's wife spoke up and said, "Never mind him, officer. He always talks this way when he's drunk."

☛ The sheriff approached the woman swimming stark naked in the village pond and said, "Pardon, Miss, but swimming isn't allowed here."

"Well," she said, "why didn't you tell me before I undressed?"

The sheriff said, "Well, there ain't no law against undressing."

☞ A state trooper in a helicopter spotted a speeder and radioed a patrol car on the ground. The patrolman stopped the speeding automobile and the driver was a bit uncertain as to how his speeding had been discovered.

"How did you know I was speeding?" the offender asked.

As he scribbled out the ticket, the patrolman pointed skyward.

The driver looked astonished and exclaimed, "You mean He's against me, too?"

☞ As the detective took notes on the missing person's case, the wife said, "Well, actually, my husband must have been missing for nearly a week now, but I didn't really notice it until payday."

☞ Farmer Wayne went to apply for a job as deputy sheriff in town. The sheriff said, "I'll have to ask you a few questions. Which days of the week start with 'T?'

Wayne said, "Today and tomorrow."

The sheriff said, "You'd better go home and study."

The next day, Wayne came back. The sheriff asked, "Who killed Abe Lincoln?"

"No idea," Wayne answered.

"Well, go home and find out," said the sheriff.

Wayne went home and walked in the door. His wife asked, "Did you get the job?"

"I guess so," said Wayne, "they've got me working on a murder case already."

☞ No one gets paid for being disagreeable except a traffic cop, and he doesn't get many Christmas presents.

☞ The angry motorist said, "And just what am I supposed to do with this speeding ticket?"

The policeman said, "Keep it. When you get three, you win a bicycle."

☞ Following the accident in the city, the farmer said to the police officer, "He hit my car going the wrong way on a one-way street but you say it's my fault! Why?"

The officer replied, "Because his father is mayor, his brother is chief of police and I'm engaged to his sister."

☞ A vacationing farm family drove on the busy interstate highway during the afternoon rush hour. The farmer was bewildered by the missile-like speed of the other cars. But he drove at his usual rate, much slower than the minimum speed.

After a while a highway patrolman overtook him and had him pull over to the side of the road. "I suppose you know why I stopped you," the officer said.

"Sure do," the farmer replied, "I'm the only one you could catch."

☞ A farm woman walked into the police station to report her husband missing and described him as "29 years old, 6 feet, 3 inches, black hair and handsome."

"Wait a minute," said the rural desk sergeant. "I know your husband. He's bald, fat and 46 years old!"

"I know," she answered, "but who wants him back?"

☞ A local farm wife was so busy trying to complete a sweater that she was even knitting while she was driving her car. A police officer noticed her car was weaving down the street. He pulled alongside her, turned down his window and said, "Pull over."

Keeping one hand on the wheel, the woman held up the unfinished sweater and shot back, "No, cardigan."

☞ The highway patrolman was checking the license of the driver he'd stopped. "It says here you're supposed to be wearing glasses."

"But officer," he replied, "I have contacts."

The patrolman replied, "I don't care who you know, you're under arrest."

☞ On a curving road in a rural area, two farmers crashed their pickup trucks head-on. While the two men were exchanging license and registration numbers, one man said to the other, "You seem a little shaken up. How about a drink?"

The drink was accepted gratefully. After a few swallows, the other driver said to his host, "Aren't you going to have one yourself?"

"Not now," said the first farmer. "Not until after the police get here."

☞ A wildly excited man ran into the police station shouting, "I need help! A man just stole my car!"

"Did you see him?" asked the desk officer.

"No," he said, struggling for breath, "but I got the license number as he pulled away."

☞ A woman woman went to the police to report her husband missing. "He's bald and skinny, has no teeth and no personality," she said. "In fact, most of him was missing before he was."

☞ A burglar broke into the home of a modern artist. The artist, however, caught a glimpse of the thief and made a sketch for the police.

Within a few hours, thanks to the sketch, the police had booked two vultures, a rusty tractor, a gorilla, three large baskets of fruit and a Russian wolfhound.

☞ A fellow who had one drink too many was driving the wrong way on a one-way street and was hailed by a cop who rasped, "Hey, didn't you see the arrows?"

"Honest, officer," the man slurred, "I didn't even see the Indians!"

☞ A man telephoned the police station to say that his steering wheel, brake pedal and accelerator had been stolen. Before the police could investigate, the phone rang again. It was the same man.

"Don't bother coming," he said as soberly as he could manage. "I got into the back seat by mistake."

☞ With a grinding of brakes, the officer pulled up his squad car and shouted to a little boy playing in the field, "Say, sonny, have you seen an airplane come down anywhere near here?"

"No, sir," replied the boy, trying to hide his b.b. gun. "I've only been shooting at that bottle on the fence."

☞ The police officer helped the battered man up from the pavement in front of the local hangout and asked, "Can you describe the man who hit you?"

The man got a frightened look on his face and said, "That's exactly what I was doing when he hit me!"

☞ Mrs. Jones is a very large woman. Besides her great number of pounds, she is unusually timid about crossing streets where the traffic is heavy. One day she stopped a policeman in the middle of the street.

"Officer," she asked, "could you see me across the street?"

The officer turned and regarded her closely. "Madam," he replied, "I could see you for half a block."

☞ The farmer had just been pulled over to the curb for speeding. The officer, pad in hand, approached the car.

"OK, you," snapped the officer. "What's your name?"

"Aloysius Gloustershire Merkowitzskyvitch III," the driver replied.

"Well," the cop said, pocketing his notebook, "don't let me catch you again."

☞ At the police station, Howard asked, "Could I see the man who was arrested for robbing our house last night?

The desk sergeant asked, "This is pretty unusual. Why do you want to see him?"

"I don't mind telling you," Howard said. "I only want to ask how he got in the house without waking my wife."

☞ "You were brought in for drinking," the desk sergeant explained.

The man let out a sigh of relief. "Great!" he said with a smile. "That's different. When do we start?"

Deep In The Heart Of Texas

"It's easy to pick out a rich Texan—he's the guy who doesn't know whose picture is on the $1 bill."

Chapter 43

The Lone Star State

"I think the children are old enough now," the Texan whispered to his wife. "Let's tell them about Alaska."

☛ "That, suh," the Texan drawled to the Boston visitor, "is the Alamo. There 136 Texans held off Santa Ana's 15,000-man army for four days. And that is the statue of a Texas Ranger who killed 46 Apaches and broke up 27 riots in his lifetime. I bet you never had anybody so brave around Boston."

"You know," the Bostonian said. "We have heroes up there, too. Paul Revere, for instance—"

"Paul Revere?" interrupted the Texan. "Isn't that the fella who ran for help?"

☛ A Texas woman was visiting her cousin in Oklahoma. "I don't want to brag," the Texan said, "but my husband just gave me an ice-maker for Christmas."

Her cousin looked at her, surprised, and said, "Mary Beth, lots of people get ice-makers."

She replied, "Sure, but Alaska?"

☛ A prominent Houston oil man and cattle rancher caught his eight-year-old son, Tyler, lighting a cigarette with a $1,000 bill.

"How many times," the enraged father shouted, "have I told you—you're too young to smoke!"

☛ A posse had just captured a horse thief and was preparing to string him up. One member of the crowd spoke up, "May I say a prayer for this man?"

The deputy in charge of the posse protested vigorously. "Are you trying to sneak this here varmint into Heaven when he ain't even fit to live in Texas?"

☞ On a cruise up the Alaskan coast, two senators, one from Texas and one from Alaska, were arguing about the size and importance of their respective states. The Texan wouldn't budge, claiming the Lone Star State didn't bow down to Alaska in anything—not size, scenery, resources or citizens.

As they debated, a giant iceberg loomed ahead. The Texan stopped, studied it a moment, then conceded: "Well, I've got to admit, you do have bigger ice cubes."

☞ A Texas rancher's wife called to her husband, "Will you get the car out, Tex, and drive the kids to the backyard so they can play?"

☞ A visitor was bragging about his tiny sports car to a rich Texan. After speaking about its economical gas mileage, speed and looks, he was winded.

"You don't have to convince me, son," the Texan said. "Almost every oil man in Texas owns a sports car."

The man said, "Really? I thought all Texans drove big Cadillacs. Why would you need sports cars?"

The Texan replied, "To stand on when we wash our Cadillacs."

☞ A Texan who got to brooding over the fact that he was living in only the second largest state went up to Alaska and asked, "How do I get to be an Alaskan?"

The bartender in the Last Chance Saloon, figuring to have a little fun with the southern blowhard, said, "Partner, you can't be a full-blooded Alaskan until you've downed a pint of whiskey in one gulp, made love to an Eskimo and shot a polar bear."

"That's for me," the Texan drawled, planking down some cash and ordering the nearest pint of whiskey. He got it down in one gulp although his eyes were glazing slightly as he stumbled out of the saloon.

The boys at the bar waited for him until past midnight, when he crashed through the doors all scratched and ripped and bloody.

"OK," he said, "OK, I'm gonna be an Alaskan. Now where's this Eskimo I'm supposed to shoot?"

☞ A Texan was dictating his will. "To my son, Junior, I leave $3 million—and he's lucky I didn't cut him off entirely."

☛ When a Texas elementary school class was told that the next day they would learn to draw, 18 youngsters showed up with pistols.

☛ A New Yorker, who spent a short vacation on a Texas ranch, returned home, bringing his wife several fur coats, a Cadillac and pockets of cash.

"How were you able to get all these things?" his wife asked.

"Shoot, honey," he replied, "I was in Houston during Halloween and I went out trick-or-treating."

☛ A wealthy Texan had a debutante party for his daughter and invited 50 eligible young men to the event. In his Olympic-sized swimming pool were 23 hungry, snapping alligators and crocodiles. "I've got $1 million for the first boy to swim the length of the pool," he said.

"And if that doesn't motivate you fellas enough, then I'll give you 10,000 acres of ranch land which includes the house and yard where you are now standing.

"Or, I'll give you the hand of my beautiful daughter, Darlene, in marriage, who is our only heir. So whoever takes her will eventually get our fortune."

Just as he finished, there was a loud splash in the south end of the pool. The Texas rancher was elated that someone accepted his challenge and said, "What do you want?"

As the boy climbed out of the pool, he said, "What I really want is the name of that bum who pushed me in the pool."

☛ Shortly after Alaska became the 49th state, a skeptical Texan visited the new state to see if things up there really were bigger than in Texas. Browsing around Anchorage, he noticed a farm-supply warehouse stocked with gigantic stacks of chicken wire. The Texan spoke up to one of the warehouse workers.

"In Texas, the chickens are so big," the Texan bragged, "that chicken wire won't hold 'em. We don't have any use for chicken wire."

"Oh, that's not chicken wire," the Alaskan replied. "That's our mosquito netting."

☛ Not all Texans are bad. There's a little boy from Dallas who says when he grows up he wants to go to Beverly Hills to do missionary work among the poor.

☛ Two Texas ranchers were talking. One complained to his friend that his delinquent son was heading for a career in crime. "I know I've neglected him," the father confessed, "and that may be the reason—but what can I do?"

"Why don't you buy him a present?" the friend suggested.

"I've thought of that," he said, "but what do you buy for a kid who has everything?"

"Well," suggested his companion, "if it were me, I'd buy him the city police department."

☛ Elmer, a mechanic in a very small town in Nebraska, dropped his name in a raffle box and was the grand prize winner of a trip to Texas. Everyone in town was very excited for him, and people were constantly telling him how everything was so big in the Lone Star State.

As soon as he arrived in Texas, he went downtown to get a beer, and he was handed a big pail of beer. Golly, he thought, my friends were right—even the beer is big in Texas.

After a few hours and one too many beers, Elmer stumbled out of the bar and attempted to walk back to his hotel. In his drunken stupor, however, he wandered aimlessly into a well-to-do residential neighborhood.

Unable to see an Olympic-sized swimming pool that lay ahead of him, Elmer toppled into the water. Suddenly waking, he screamed in a frenzy, "Please, don't flush!"

☛ A loaded Texas rancher purchased his first Rolls-Royce. About a week after it had been delivered, he took it back to the dealer to complain that strange wheezing noises were emanating from the front end of the car.

"There's only one possible explanation," said the dealer after looking it over, "your chauffeur must have asthma."

☛ A hitchhiker was picked up by a wealthy Texan driving a big expensive Cadillac. Seeing a pair of horn-rimmed glasses on the seat between them, the hitchhiker remarked, "Do you need glasses while you're driving, sir?"

"No more, son," the Texan remarked. "I had the whole doggone windshield ground to my prescription."

☛ Although nobody really knows it, George Washington actually lived in Texas. He chopped down a mesquite tree. When his father asked who had chopped down the tree, little

George said, "I cannot tell a lie. I chopped down the mesquite tree with my little hatchet."

"If you can't tell a lie, son," the elder Washington said, "then you ain't got no business in Texas."

☞ During a convention luncheon in Chicago, a loudmouth Texan was bragging about being an expert on drinks. As he boasted, a colleague slipped out and brought back a glass of colorless liquid.

"OK," he told the braggart, "take a swallow of this and tell us what it is."

The bigmouth Texan took a sizable swig, then sputtering and choking, he said, "That's gasoline."

"Yeah, we know," said the other fellow, "but is it premium or regular?"

☞ A senator from Alaska was ribbing a Texas senator about the fact that Alaska's admission to the Union reduced Texas to second rank in size.

"If you don't shut your trap," the Texas senator warned, "a few Texans will come to your state and throw a cocktail party. When they're through using your ice, you'll be smaller than Rhode Island."

☞ An Illinois farmer was surprised in speaking to a rich Texas rancher to learn that he owned a Volkswagen. When he asked him why he drove the Volkswagen, the Texan replied, "Because I have insomnia and I've discovered that by driving a few hours before I go to bed, I rest better."

"But with your money," said the Illinois native, "why don't you drive a Cadillac?"

The Texan looked at him funny and said, "In my bedroom?"

☞ A rich Texan bragged about his 14-year-old son, Troy, who owned 7,000 acres and 300 cows. "And the best part of it is that the kid earned it all by himself," he added.

Someone in the group spoke up and asked, "How on earth did a kid earn all that at only 14 years of age?"

The Texan replied proudly, "Well, he got four A's and one B on his report card."

In God We Trust

"Americans are a religious people. You can tell they trust in God by the way they drive."

Chapter 44

Those Sleepy
Sermon Listeners

*"Don't stay away from church
because there are so many hypocrites.
There's always room for one more."*
—A.R. Adams

☛ A western rancher who was speeding too fast along the mountain road shot over the edge at a corner. Luckily, the top on the convertible was down and the driver managed to grab hold of a stunted tree as the car dropped thousands of feet into the canyon.

"Help," he called, as he hung on, dangling above the canyon. "Can anyone hear me?"

All he heard was an echo. "God, can you hear me?" he called, looking at the sky.

The clouds rolled together and a deep voice said, "Yes, I can hear you."

"Will you help me?"

"Yes," God answered, "I will help you. Do you believe in me?"

"Yes," the rancher answered, "I believe in you."

"Do you trust me?"

"Yes, yes, I trust you," the farmer said again. "But hurry up."

"If you trust me," God said, "let go of the tree."

After a long silence, the rancher yelled, "Can anyone else hear me?"

☛ A retired farmer in the second pew had fallen asleep during the Sunday morning sermon. Midway through the sermon on the wages of sin, the preacher pounded on the lectern and shouted, "Anyone who wants to go to Hell, stand up!"

The farmer, hearing only the words, "stand up," looked

around with a puzzled expression as he stood alone. "Preacher," he said, "I don't know what we're voting on, but it looks like you and I are the only ones for it."

☛ The rural pastor, looking over the unusually large Easter congregation, announced, "Dear parishioners, I realize that I shall not see many of you again until next Easter so permit me to take this opportunity to wish you all a very Merry Christmas and a most prosperous New Year."

☛ Two hobos were walking down the street one morning when they met a Catholic priest with his arm in a sling. They chatted for a moment when one of the hobos asked the priest what happened to his arm. The priest told them he had the misfortune to slip and fall while getting out of the bathtub.
"What's a bathtub?" one hobo asked as they continued their walk.
The other replied, "How should I know? I'm not Catholic."

☛ An old farmer was on his deathbed and a preacher came by to read him his last rites. "Brother Wilson," the preacher said, "are you willing to denounce the devil?"
The clergyman was surprised by the reply. "No, I ain't," the old man said. "I don't figure I'm in any position to be making enemies."

☛ A small town minister asked one of his parishioners, "Shall I give you something to strengthen your will power?"
"No," said the poor, consulting soul, "give me something to weaken my conscience instead."

☛ The preacher paid a duty call at the rural home of a sick member of his parish. After a little while he decided to read aloud a few verses of scripture and asked the family for a Bible.
The sick woman called to her little daughter in the next room, "Darling," she said in a syrupy voice, "would you get that old book your mother loves so well."
The little girl promptly returned with the Sears & Roebuck mail-order catalog.

☛ In a rural parish, there was a young priest who was a terrific sports nut. On Super Bowl Sunday, he was torn between watching the game and hearing confessions, so he compromised and took a radio with him into the confessional booth.

All was going well until a young woman entered the booth, made her confession and met a friend soon after. Noticing the young woman shaking her head in bewilderment, the friend asked, "What's the matter?"

"I just went to confession," the young woman said, "and I got 15 yards for rushing the passer."

☞ The minister's sermon concerned the relationship between fact and faith. "That you are sitting before me in this church," he said, "is fact. That I am standing, speaking from this pulpit, is fact.

"But it is only faith that makes me believe anyone is listening to me."

☞ As the tour boat was sinking, the skipper called out, "Does anyone here know how to pray?"

A vacationing farmer replied, "Yes, I do."

"OK, go ahead and pray," the captain said. "The rest of us will put on life jackets. We're one short."

☞ A group of farmers were suffering through a severe drought. Finally, they went to their new minister and asked him to hold a special service at the church so they could all pray for rain.

Well, the service was held and they had no more than said, "Amen" when it started raining cats and dogs. It kept on raining harder and harder until it washed out the crops and all the farmers were ruined.

One old-timer said, "Well, that's what comes from trusting such a request to a minister who doesn't know anything about agriculture."

☞ A farmer was finishing his haying one Sunday morning when the pastor of the local church drove by. "Brother," the minister lectured, "don't you know the Creator made the world in six days and rested on the seventh?"

"Yes," the farmer said as he looked uneasily at the rain clouds in the sky. "I know all about that. But He got done and I didn't."

☞ The pastor said to a farmer named Jake, "You claim you can't donate because you owe everybody. Don't you feel you

238

owe the Lord something?"

Jake answered, "Yes, but He isn't pushing me like the rest are."

☛ A Catholic girl fell in love with a Jewish boy. Her mother, a devout religious woman said, "He loves you, so just convince him to convert and become Catholic."

Two weeks later, the girl came home and announced that she had converted him and the wedding date was set.

But two weeks later, she came home in tears, saying the wedding was off. "But why?" asked the mother. "You said everything was fine and he agreed to convert."

The girl said, "Yes, but I guess I oversold him—now he wants to become a priest!"

☛ In a California state mental hospital, patients were being shuffled into the Catholic and Protestant chapels. One patient, however, didn't stop at either chapel and continued walking straight for the front gate. An attendant ran out after him and asked him where he was going.

The patient replied, "I was told I could go to the church of my choice. It's in New York."

☛ One day in town a farmer by the name of Toby was stopped by the pastor of the church he attended. During their conversation, the pastor asked the man if he smoked, drank or cursed.

Toby replied hesitantly, "Well, yes, every once in a while."

The pastor, his voice full of compassion, said, "Now Brother Toby, I don't smoke, I don't drink and I don't curse."

To this, Toby said with all seriousness, "Yes sir, pastor, but you don't farm."

☛ Two farmers, fishing on a Sunday morning, were feeling a little guilty about skipping church. One said to the other, "I suppose we should've gone to church."

"I couldn't have gone to church anyway," the second said. "My wife is extremely sick in bed."

☛ Farming wasn't going too well in a certain Alabama community. A preacher was asked by his congregation to pray for a more abundant crop.

The preacher said, "O, Lord, we pray thee in accordance with the request of this, thy people, that thou send them a more abundant crop; but O, Lord, thou knowest as they know, that what they need is deeper plowing, harder work and more manure."

☛ A minister announced there were 726 different kinds of sin. Now, he is being besieged with requests for the list, mostly from folks who think they're missing something!

☛ "Folks," the old Baptist minister said, "The subject of my sermon this evening is liars. How many in this congregation have read the 69th chapter of Matthew?"
Nearly every hand in the audience was raised.
"That's right," said the preacher. "You folks are the ones I want to preach to. There isn't any 69th chapter of Matthew."

☛ A rural parish priest was visiting with a missionary priest when the missionary asked, "So, how are things going in your parish?"
"Oh, I have a 100% active congregation," the priest replied. "They're all active fishers, or active golfers, or active swimmers, or active bowlers or..."

☛ During the great flood, Noah's Ark sprang a leak and Noah sent a dog to plug the hole. All he did was put his nose in it. Noah then sent a woman to fix the problem, but all she did was step on it. Still unable to find a solution, he sent a man to do the job but all he did was sit on it.
Ever since, all dogs have cold noses, all women have cold feet and men have sat on their butts.

☛ A customer came into the country bank to open a Christmas Club account.
"In what denomination?" the bank teller asked.
The puzzled customer replied, "Lutheran."

☛ A circuit preacher, making his rounds on horseback through the hill country, passed an old woman in the parish, contentedly puffing on a corncob pipe on the porch of her shack.
Pointing an accusing finger at the offending pipe, the preacher asked, "Mabel, do you expect to be saved?"
She answered that yes, indeed, she did expect salvation.
"Well," the preacher's voice rose, "don't you know, woman, that the Bible says nothing unclean shall enter Heaven? How

do you expect to go there with your breath smelling of evil tobacco?"

"Well, Reverend," Mabel replied, "when I die, I 'spect to leave my breath behind."

☛ A minister offered some strong horseradish to a new parish guest who took a big bite and then gasped, "I've heard many ministers preach hell-fire, but you're the first one I've met who passed out samples."

☛ The rural minister arose to address his congregation. "There is a certain man among us today who is flirting with another man's wife," he said. "Unless he puts $5 in the collection box, his name will be read from the pulpit."

When the collection plate came back, the ushers counted 19 $5 bills and a $2 bill with this note attached: "Other $3 when I get my milk check."

☛ A country pastor complained to a farmer about his absence from church the previous Sunday. "I had haying to do," the farmer explained, "and it was over in the back lot where nobody could see me working on the Sabbath."

"But God saw you," the pastor protested.

"I know it," the farmer burst out, "but He's not so gossipy as the people around here."

☛ Don't ever doubt that God has a sense of humor. You're here, aren't you?

☛ One Sunday morning, as a beggar stood on a corner holding out his hat, a woman stopped and glared at him. "If you went to church," she scolded, "maybe you would be more fortunate."

"You're wrong, lady," replied the beggar. "I passed my hat around at church last Sunday, and they threw me out."

☛ A minister was talking to the town drunk who also had a reputation as a woman-chaser. "You ought to taper off a little, Ray," said the minister. "Which would you rather give up, wine or women?"

The drunk thought for a moment. "Well," he said, "it would depend on the vintage."

☛ A rural minister, discovering at the last minute that he'd forgotten to invite a little old lady to his garden party, called her up and asked her to come.

"It's too late," she said. "I've already prayed for rain."

☛ An old codger guided his car around a sharp curve and happened to run his minister off the side of the road and down a canyon. The old-timer hobbled down to the car and asked, "Pastor, are you hurt? Are you all right?"

The minister replied, "I'm fine, thank goodness. The Lord was with me."

The old man said, "Well, you better let Him ride with me— you're going to kill Him driving that way."

☛ A farmer who had driven his mules to town one morning arrived back at the farm that evening three hours late.

"What took you so long?" his wife asked.

"On the way back home," the farmer explained, "I picked up the minister, and from then on, them mules didn't understand a thing I said!"

☛ There has been little real progress in the last 6,000 years of history. It took Noah 40 days just to find a parking space.

☛ "Do you think of yourself as a soldier in the army of the Lord?" the priest asked a farmer in his parish.

"Yes, I do," the farmer said.

"Then why do I only see you at Christmas and Easter?" the priest asked.

"I'm in the secret service," the farmer quickly replied.

☛ A bull-headed parishioner objected to some church improvements. The minister had said he wanted to start with the purchase of a new chandelier.

When the pastor asked why the parishioner objected, he stated, "Well, first, no one can spell it. Second, no one can play it. And third, what we really need around here is more light."

☛ A visiting TV evangelist had a very receptive crowd in a rural community, and he scanned the group for a likely candidate to be his best example. He settled on an elderly farmer sitting in the front row. The preacher stood before the man, placed his hand on his head and asked, "Are you ready to denounce the devil and all his evil ways?"

"Yep," replied the man.

The preacher continued, "Are you willing to forsake all your sins?"

Again, the man nodded in agreement and the evangelist went on. "Are you ready to pay all your debts?" he asked.

There was a pause before the man shook his head and sharply replied, "We've been talkin' about religion, but now you're talkin' about business."

☛ The church service was proceeding successfully when an attractive young widow, seated in the balcony, leaned too far and fell over the railing. Her dress caught the chandelier and she was suspended upside down in mid-air.

The minister noticed her undignified position and thundered, "Any person who looks will be stricken blind!"

A farmer whispered to the man next to him, "I'm going to risk one eye."

Chapter 45

Men Of The Cloth

*"A church is a place in which
the gentlemen who have never
been to Heaven brag about it to
people who will never get there."*
—*H.L. Mencken*

☛ A minister who had been at the parish for a few years, resigned to go to another church. Following the benediction, a lady replied, "Pastor, what are we going to do without you?"

Trying to comfort her, he searched for the right words. "My dear friend, in this church the bishop always sends someone to carry on and do a better job than his predecessor."

"Oh no, don't say that," the woman said. "They told us the same thing when our last pastor resigned and they sent you."

☛ A mountain woman, attending church in the foothills, stood up in the pew to leave when her baby began to shriek. "Stop, my good woman," the preacher said. "Your innocent little babe's crying doesn't disturb me."

Turning in the aisle, the mother replied, "That may be, Mr. Preacher, but you're a'disturbin' him."

☛ A man in the passenger train car asked for something from the porter that couldn't be supplied. He then called out, "Is there a Catholic priest in the car?"

No one answered. "Is there an Episcopalian minister in the car?" he asked.

Still, no one answered.

A voice finally spoke up. "If you need spiritual comfort, I'm a Methodist minister," someone volunteered.

"I don't want spiritual comfort," the man said. "I want a corkscrew."

☛ Outside church one day, a youngster named Brett piped up, "You know what? I'm going to be a minister when I grow up."

"That's just fine," the reverend said. "But what made you decide to become a minister?"

"Well," Brett said thoughtfully. "I'll have to go to church on Sunday anyway, and I think it'd be more fun to stand up and holler like you than it is sitting still and listening."

☛ The hat was passed in a tight-fisted country congregation one morning. It returned to the altar almost empty.

"Oh, Lord," the preacher said, "I thank thee that I got my hat back."

☛ A minister of a local church became increasingly concerned about what women were wearing or not wearing to his Sunday service. To clear up the problem, he began standing in front of the church screening people as they came in.

One particular Sunday, a topless dancer from a cocktail bar down the street approached the church in her "uniform."

The minister said, "You're not coming in here like that."

The dancer replied, "I don't know why not. After all, I have a divine right."

"I notice you also have a divine left," the minister said, "but you aren't coming in here like that."

☛ "I have stolen a chicken," the conscience-stricken parishioner said to his rural pastor. "Would you care to have it?"

"Certainly not!" replied the pastor sternly. "I can't accept stolen goods! You must return it to the one from whom you stole it."

"But," said the parishioner, "I have offered it to him and he refused it."

"In that case," the pastor said, "you might as well keep it yourself."

"Thank you, sir," said the man, as he hurried away.

When the pastor returned home that evening, he found one of his chickens missing.

☛ A panel of theologians was discussing the burning question of when life begins. "Life begins," said the Catholic priest, "at the moment of conception."

"No, no Father," the Presbyterian minister said, "Life begins at the moment of birth."

Both turned to the aging Jewish rabbi. "Life begins," the

rabbi said, slowly stroking his beard, "when the kids leave home and the dog dies."

☛ Three kids were arguing at the playground. The first, a doctor's son, said, "My pop makes money easy. All he does is look at a person, talks to him, writes something down and gets $50."

A lawyer's son then bragged, "That's nothing. My pop sits in his office, someone comes in, he tells them to look it up in a book and he gets $75."

Just then, a rural minister's son piped up, "Oh, but my dad gets up, talks and it takes six men to bring the money down the aisles."

☛ After serving for many years as pastor of a small country church, the minister found it was time for him to move on to a larger church and a larger congregation.

During his last Sunday sermon to the people of his church, the minister told his followers, "It is the same God that brought me here that is taking me to a new church."

At that moment, the church choir piped up and sang, "What a Friend We Have in Jesus."

☛ At the close of his sermon, the preacher discovered one of his deacons sound asleep and snoring. To teach him a lesson, he announced, "Now, we will have a few minutes of prayer. Deacon Brown will lead."

"Lead?" said the groggy Deacon Brown, suddenly awakening, "I just dealt."

☛ An explorer was hiking through the African jungle when he stumbled upon a fierce-looking tribe. "Does your tribe know anything about religion?" he asked.

The chief spoke up and said, "Well, we had a taste of it when the last missionary was here."

☛ The young widow White stopped attending Sunday church and Wednesday night prayer meetings after her husband died. Finally, she showed up one Sunday.

The preacher, as was his custom when he finished his sermon, stood at the church door shaking everybody's hand as they filed out of church. Along came widow White and the preacher grasped and patted her hand warmly as he said in his most solicitous manner, "Widow White, it's so good to see you. I prayed for you last night."

The attractive young widow looked him straight in the eye and replied, "My God, why didn't you call? I could've been there in 10 minutes."

☞ Reverend Thomas entered church one Sunday and found several letters awaiting him. He opened one and found it contained only the single word, "Fool." During his service that morning he announced to his congregation:

"I have known many an instance of a man writing a letter and forgetting to sign his name, but this is the only instance I have ever known of a man signing his name and forgetting to write the letter."

☞ A farmer walking downtown was stopped by the minister's wife. "We've missed seeing you in church lately," she said politely.

"After all, a man doesn't have to go to church to be a good Christian, does he?" the farmer hedged.

"No," answered the clergyman's wife. "He doesn't. And a woman doesn't have to be married to be a mother either, but most people seem to think it's a good idea."

☞ A young clergyman, sent as an assistant to a rural parish, was worried about his lack of experience in country matters. He decided that perhaps he could make a start by teaching himself how to milk a cow.

Seizing a bucket and stool, he approached a cow in the middle of the field and set to work. The cow had other ideas, however, and moved off. The young minister followed.

When this had happened several times, a friend who was watching from the road, shouted to the clergyman, "What are you doing?"

Back came the reply, "About three miles to the gallon."

☞ The priest was giving his Sunday sermon on poverty, and somehow he got back to his favorite subject—his lousy wages. Right in the middle, he said, "I make $100 a week and that's not enough!"

The assistant priest followed with, "I make $60 a week and that's not enough!"

Then the organist got into the act and started singing with a smile, "I make $500 a week...There's no business like show business..."

☛ A woman was sitting next to a clergyman on a plane. She became increasingly nervous as the jet ran into thunder squalls and was buffeted by severe downdrafts and cross-winds.

After one particularly alarming air pocket tossed them about, she looked at the minister and said, "Please, Reverend, can't you do something that will stop this storm and save our lives?"

"I'm sorry, ma'am," he replied, "but I'm connected with sales, not with management."

☛ Two priests were talking at the church festival. "Hey, I just heard another one," one said. "What's black and white and glows in the dark?"

The other priest shrugged his shoulders.

"A nun from Three Mile Island!" the priest roared.

☛ One Sunday, after the pastor had been talking in his sermon about the lion and the lamb living together in peace, a circus man in the congregation came up to argue that the arrangement couldn't possibly work.

"Well," said the preacher, "Why don't we try it? You get a lion and I will get one of my farmer members to bring in a lamb."

The circus man got a cage and a lion and they put them on the church lawn. He left town before the farmer brought in the lamb, but when he returned three weeks later, sure enough, the lion and the lamb were lying down together in peace.

"Well," said the pastor, "It works fine, but we have to replace the lamb once in a while."

☛ A psychiatrist talked to his patient on the couch. "Do you talk in your sleep?"

"No, I talk in other people's sleep," the patient said.

"Wait a second," the shrink said. "I don't understand. How can that be?"

The patient answered, "I'm a preacher."

☛ The pastor of a church on the outskirts of town phoned the local board of health to ask that a dead mule be removed from the yard out in front of his house. The smart-aleck clerk thought he'd be clever and said, "I thought you clergymen took care of the dead."

"We do," remarked the pastor, "but we get in touch with

their relatives first."

☞ After a rural preacher died and was standing in line to enter the Pearly Gates, he noticed a dirty, grungy man wearing soiled blue jeans who was allowed to go in before him.

"I don't understand," the preacher said, turning to St. Peter. "Why—that's a cab driver from New Orleans! I devoted my entire life to my congregation. Why should he go in before me?"

"Our policy is to reward results," St. Peter explained. "Now what happened, Reverend, whenever you gave a sermon?"

The minister admitted some people in his congregation occasionally dozed off.

"Exactly," St. Peter said. "And when people rode in this man's taxi, they not only stayed awake, they prayed!"

☞ The sermon seemed to go on forever. Finally, the minister paused and asked, "What more, my friends, can I possibly say?"

From the back of the church came a roaring reply, "Amen!"

☞ The pit boss at a Las Vegas casino found the Lord and left to take a job with a church in Nebraska as assistant to the minister. After a few weeks, he sought an opinion from his employer.

The minister said, "Carl, you're doing fine, real fine. But there's just one thing. We like to refer to it as the collection, not the take."

☞ The wife of a rural clergyman died. Naturally, he wished to be relieved of his duties for a few days, so he sent a message to the bishop's office. However, the bishop was a bit surprised when he received the following message:

"I regret to inform you that my wife has just died, and I should be obliged if you could send me a substitute for the weekend."

☞ The new minister's car broke down just after the morning service, so on Monday he drove it to the local garage for repairs.

"I hope you'll go easy on the price, my son," he told the mechanic. "After all, I'm just a poor preacher."

"I know," the mechanic said. "I've heard you."

☛ A wealthy farmer decided to go to church on Easter. After the services, he approached the minister with great enthusiasm. "Reverend," he said, "that was a #&%$@ good sermon!"

"I'm grateful," the minister replied, "that you were pleased with it, but it would be nice if you didn't use those terms to express yourself."

"I can't help it," said the farmer. "I still think it was a #&%$@ good sermon, and I was so moved by it that I put $100 in the collection basket."

"The @$%&# you did!" said the minister.

☛ One cold, blustery Sunday at a country church, just two people arrived for services—the pastor and one parishioner.

"No one else is coming," said the pastor, "so we won't have a service today."

"Well, I'm a farmer," the man said, "and if just one cow comes up, I feed her."

So the pastor went ahead with the regular songs, announcements, prayers and a long sermon. When it was over, he asked the man if he had enjoyed the sermon.

"I'm a farmer," the man said, "and if one cow comes up, I feed her. But I don't dump the whole load of feed on her."

Chapter 46

Sunday School Days

"The only thing a kid wants to get out of Sunday School is himself."

☞ A Sunday School class was being quizzed on the prodigal son. The teacher asked one youngster, "Who was sorry when the prodigal son returned home?"

The boy gave it a lot of deep thought and said, "The fatted calf."

☞ A church that loved good fellowship always served coffee and doughnuts after the sermon. The pastor asked a little boy if he knew why they served coffee.

"I think," the boy said, "it's to get the people wide awake before they drive home."

☞ A Sunday School teacher asked her preschool class if they knew where God lived. One boy stood up and quietly said, "He lives in Heaven."

"Is that correct, Becky?" the teacher asked a little girl in the back row.

"No, ma'am," said the girl. "He lives in the bathroom at our house."

"The bathroom?"

"Sure," Becky said. "Every morning my dad stands outside the door and shouts, 'My God, are you still in there?'"

☞ A little tot, with his parents in church for the first time, watched the ushers pass the collection plates. When they neared his pew, he piped up loudly, "Don't pay for me, Daddy. I'm under five."

☞ A 10-year-old farm boy was telling his mother what he'd learned at Sunday School.

"Well, our teacher told us about when God sent Moses

behind the enemy lines to rescue the Israelites from the Egyptians. When they came to the Red Seas, Moses called for engineers to build a pontoon bridge. After they crossed, they looked back and saw the Egyptian tanks coming. Quick as a flash, Moses radioed headquarters on his walkie-talkie to send bombers to blow up the bridge and saved the Israelites."

"T.J.," exclaimed his startled mother, "is that really the way your teacher told the story?"

"Well, not exactly. But if I told it her way, you'd never believe it!"

☛ While little Danny knelt beside the bed and began saying his prayers, his mother said, "Speak up, son. I can't hear you."

"I wasn't talking to you," Danny snapped.

☛ The Sunday School teacher asked Bobby why he was late. "I was gonna go fishing this morning," said Bobby, "but Daddy wouldn't let me."

"You're a very fortunate boy to have a father like that," said the teacher. "And did your father make it clear to you why you shouldn't go fishing on Sunday?"

"Oh, sure," Bobby replied. "He said there wasn't enough bait for both of us."

☛ A preacher came out of the country church where three little boys were standing. The preacher asked if they wanted to go to Heaven. Two of the boys said, "Yes," but the other remained silent.

The preacher said, "You mean you are not going to Heaven when you die?"

"Oh," said the boy, "I thought you were getting a truckload to go right now."

☛ At Sunday School, Alex was deeply impressed by the story of Eve's creation from one of Adam's ribs. Later in the day, after running too hard on the farm, he felt a pain in his side.

"Oh," he gasped, "I think I'm going to have a wife."

☛ A five-year-old boy was playing with the small daughter of the new neighbors. They had been wading in the pond and finally decided the only way to keep their clothes dry was to take them off.

As they were going back into the water, the little boy looked the girl over and remarked, "Gosh, I didn't know there was that much difference between Catholics and Protestants."

☞ Scott, getting a bit philosophical, asked his mother, "Are there liars in Heaven, Mom?"

She answered, "No, Scott, what makes you ask?"

"Well, I was just thinking," Scott said. "Wouldn't it be awful lonely with just George Washington and God up there?"

☞ Little Julia learned in Sunday School that God expects us to do more than pray and that we must help our prayers be answered. Julia's brother had made a trap to catch sparrows and she prayed that it would fail. For three days she prayed hard and at last she was smiling since she knew her prayers would be answered.

"Julia, why are you so sure your prayer will be answered?" her mother asked.

The little girl replied, "I know it will be answered because I went out there three days ago and kicked the trap to pieces."

☞ An eight-year-old boy told his mother he didn't want to go to Sunday School. "I'll bet Dad never went to Sunday School when he was a kid," the boy argued.

"Oh, yes," the mother replied. "Your father went to Sunday School regularly when he was young."

"All right," the boy finally agreed reluctantly. "But I bet it won't do me any good, either."

☞ After the Sunday School teacher had told her class a story of sacrifice from the Old Testament, she asked her pupils, "Why don't we have burnt offerings today?"

One boy raised his hand and quickly answered, "On account of air pollution."

☞ A farmer asked his wife, "Why doesn't little Katie sing in the choir anymore?"

His wife said, "She was absent one Sunday and somebody asked if the organ had been fixed."

☞ A little girl in Sunday School had a tough problem for her teacher to explain. "Last night," the girl said, "I dreamed God sneezed and I didn't know what to say."

☛ A couple of youngsters had been to Sunday School and as they walked slowly home, they talked about the devil—the subject of the lesson for the day.

"What do you think about all that devil stuff?" asked one.

"Well," mused the second, "I don't know, but I do know how the Santa Claus story turned out—the devil is probably just your dad, too!"

☛ Little Betsy was taken to church for the first time. As she walked out of church with her parents, the preacher stopped her, leaned over and asked how she liked church.

"I liked the music," Betsy said, "but the commercial was too long."

☛ A new Sunday School teacher had to iron out the problems with the Lord's Prayer.

One child had to be corrected after reciting, "Howard be thy name."

Another youngster prayed, "Lead us not into Penn Station."

Still another surprised her teacher with, "Our Father, who art in Heaven, how'd you know my name?"

☛ Following his sermon on trying to love thy neighbor as thyself, the minister stopped a little boy on the way out of church and asked, "Son, if a neighbor boy hits you on the cheek, what will you do?"

The boy replied, "How big is he?"

☛ A TV evangelist arrived in a rural town and asked a small boy where the post office was. When the boy had told him how to get there, the evangelist said, "If you'll come over to the Baptist Church tonight, you can hear me give directions for getting into Heaven."

"I don't think I'll be there," said the boy. "After all, you don't even know your way to the post office."

☛ A rural minister was lecturing the Sunday School class on the evils of sin. He turned to one youngster and asked, "Do you know where boys and girls go who do bad things?"

"Yes, sir," replied Michelle. "Behind old man Turner's barn."

☛ It was the high point of the Sunday sermon and the preacher was describing Judgment Day. "Thunder will roar, flames will shoot from the heavens, floods, storms, earthquakes will devastate the world," the preacher said.

Wide-eyed, the little boy in the fifth row turned to his mother and whispered, "Mom, will I get out of school?"

☛ The Sunday School teacher was holding her class spellbound. "Think, children," she said, "in that far-off land there are millions of square miles of land without a single Sunday School where little boys and girls can spend their Sunday mornings. Now, what should we all try to save up our money for?"

One little fellow shouted, "To go there!"

☛ The minister was on a campaign to have grace said before every meal in his parish. He stopped at one farm home and asked a small boy, "Son, do you say a prayer before every meal at your house?"

"No," replied the boy. "My mother is a good cook and we don't have to."

☛ The Sunday School teacher had concluded her lesson and wanted to make sure she had gotten her point across. "Now, who can tell me the first thing you must do to obtain forgiveness of sin?" she asked.

"Sin," replied a small voice from the back of the room.

☛ A Sunday School teacher spoke at length about the beauties of Heaven. "Now," she said, "all you children who want to go to Heaven, raise your hands."

All the hands shot up except that of one little boy.

"Why aren't you ready to go to Heaven, Doug?" the teacher asked.

"Well," he said, "when I left for Sunday School today, my mom was making apple pie."

☛ "How many times must I tell you," Mother scolded Jenny, "that we always keep our eyes closed during prayers?"

"Yes, Mommy," the child murmured. "I'm sorry." But then, after a moment's pause, she turned to mother and asked, "But how do you know that I didn't?"

☛ "Why's your Grandma always reading her Bible?" a friend asked little Steve.

"I think maybe she's studying for her finals."

☛ After attending the weekly church service, a woman with a reputation for being overly critical was talking to her neighbor. She insisted the seats in her pew were too hard, the hymns were sung off-key and the sermon was poor.

At that point, her little girl spoke up. "But, Mommy, what can you expect for a quarter?"

☛ A rural minister was calling on a parishioner one afternoon when his hostess' small son rushed in holding a giant rat by the tail.

"He's dead," he assured her. "We whacked him and slammed him and busted him until"—and then he noticed the minister—"until God called him home."

☛ A minister at the country church saw a little boy studying the scroll honoring those who died in the war. The boy asked the minister why all the names were there.

"They are the names of all the boys who died in the service."

The youth studied the names for a moment, then asked, "Which service—the 9:30 or the 11 o'clock one?"